BREAK
OUT OF THE
BOX

By
Mike Vance
and Diane Deacon

CAREER
PRESS

Franklin Lakes, NJ

Team Center™, A Kitchen for the Mind™, Grand Formatting™, Break Out of the Box™, Think Out of the Box™, Briefing Board™, Re-Potting Cycle™, MICORBS® and Displayed Thinking® are trademarks of Intellectual Equities, Inc.

Imagineering® is a trademark of the Walt Disney Company.

Questions on p. 118 excerpted from *Faces of Caring* by Val J. Halamandaris. Reprinted with permission. Copies may be obtained from Caring Publishing, 519 C Street NE, Washington, DC 20002-5809.

Letter on pp. 70-71 excerpted from *The J. Willard Marriott Story* by Robert O'Brien, © 1979 Deseret Book Company, pp. 265-267. Reprinted with permission.

BREAK OUT OF THE BOX
ISBN 1-56414-255-8, $24.99
Cover design by Ad/Art Studios
Printed in the U.S.A. by Book-mart Press

To order this title by mail, please include price as noted above, $2.50 handling per order, and $1 00 for each book ordered. Send to: Career Press, Inc., 3 Tice Road, P.O. Box 687, Franklin Lakes, NJ 07417.

Or call toll-free 1-800-CAREER-1 (NJ and Canada: 201-848-0310) to order using VISA or MasterCard, or for further information on books from Career Press.

Library of Congress Cataloging-in-Publication Data
Vance, Mike.
    Break out of the box / by Mike Vance and Diane Deacon.
        p.   cm.
    Includes index.
    ISBN 1-56414-255-8
    1. Leadership. 2. Organizational change--Management.
    3. Communication in management. 4. Management--Employee
    participation. 5. Work groups. I. Deacon, Diane, 1960-   .
    II. Title.
    HD57.7.V366   1996
    650.1--dc20   96-36311
                                                             CIP

This book is dedicated to:

our good friends

Val J. Halamandaris
and
Bill Halamandaris—

two people who understand the art
of breaking out of the box.

For further information on Mike Vance and Diane Deacon's speaking programs, seminars, recorded training programs, consulting, etc., contact:

The Creative Thinking Association of America
16600 Sprague Road
Suite #120
Cleveland, OH 44130
216-243-5576
800-535-0030
E-mail: ThinkCTA@AOL.com
Website: http://members.aol.com/vancecta/web/cta.htm

ACKNOWLEDGMENTS

Our deepest gratitude goes to the people who helped make this book possible: Ron Fry, our publisher, Brandon Toropov, who patiently translated our thoughts and ideas on many subjects to the page; Betsy Sheldon, for her extraordinary editorial skills; and special thanks to Karen Thompson and Scott Evanoff for their dedication and support in the process of making this book.

We want to thank some of our good friends who have supported and implemented our techniques and methods:

Dave Abdo	Tom Guest	Jim and Ellie Newton
Bill Anderson	David Hazen	John and Brian Palmer
Norman Brinker	Tom Hunter	Bill Peare
Larry and Robby Broedow	Mike Jenkins	Frank Ponzio
Sue Couture	Richard Kaverman	Arlyn Rayfield
Danny and Theo Cox	Jon Lee	Mike Riley
Margaret (Peg) Cushman	Karl Litzinger	Charles Ruppman
Merrill Dean	Gary Link	Eric Salama
Ken Dobler	A.C. (Mike) Markkula	Dr. Dave Savello
George and Sherry Fink	Karl May	Deb Stout
Merritt Fink	Steve McPhee	Morely Winograd
Robert Fiore	Bill Meder	Tom and Maxine Yonker

Ralph and Virginia Vance, my mother and father, who presented me with a lifetime of exemplary values and love; Mark, John and Vanessa Vance—as well as the other members of my family—who have been showing me their love since birth.

—Mike Vance

Mike Vance, my partner and my friend, who has mentored me throughout the years and taught me how to *break out of the box*, as well as Larry and Shirley Deacon, my parents, who have been both teachers and friends to me, and all of the members of my family and all of my dear friends who have given me their love.

—Diane Deacon

■ CONTENTS

On the Road to Breakthrough Thinking

"A journey of a thousand miles must begin with a single step."
—Chinese proverb

Diane Deacon was anxious about the prospect of going to another seminar, hoping, at least, the speaker was good. But her manager at the real estate office wasn't subtle about his request for her to attend this one...*no matter what.*

It didn't matter that Diane had been to quite a few seminars recently. This one was about creativity. And the tickets were nonrefundable. So Diane was going. She had pressing business to attend to, but this seminar couldn't be postponed. So, with the restrained enthusiasm of a sent person, she made her way into the large gymnasium at the local school and surveyed the rows of un-comfortable-looking metal folding chairs. Cold on the *derrière* and hard on the spine, she concluded wistfully. Just like many other seminars she had attended. She'd arrived early, as was her habit. Diane claimed a seat in the very back row next to the exit door, the better to make an early, unnoticed exit if circumstances demanded. She had attended too many seminars not to know that she shouldn't get trapped in a seat that made escape awkward. She settled into some work she'd brought along and waited for the program to get started.

Soon after, a man in a dark blue suit walked into the auditorium. After a moment, he made his way over to Diane.

"What are you doing way back here?" he asked. "The seminar's up in front."

"I've staked out this chair as an act of self-defense," Diane explained. "In case this speaker isn't any good, I'm out of here." She smiled and extended her hand to the man. They shook. "I'm Diane Deacon," she said. "Who are you?"

"Well," he answered with a smile, "I'm Mike Vance, the speaker tonight."

Then he started laughing, and Diane couldn't help joining in.

"It won't be that bad, Diane. I can guarantee it." Mike assured her. "Please come up and say hello to me after the session—assuming you decide to stick around, that is. If you do, I suppose that will be a good sign." Mike walked to the front of the room.

Soon Diane found herself leaning forward, transfixed by his message. The topic was "breaking out of the box." Mike had set up four flip charts, one featuring the following illustration:

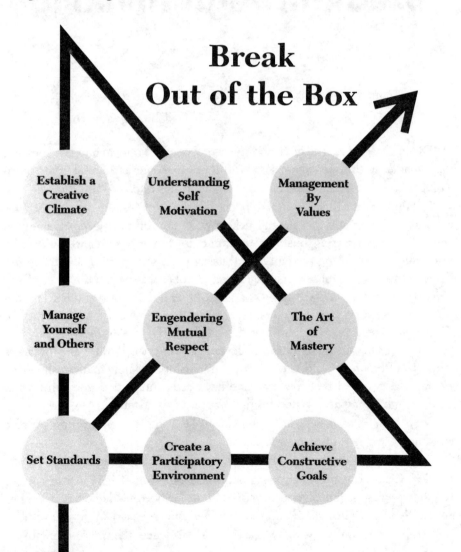

Break Out of the Box

Establish a Creative Climate

Understanding Self Motivation

Management By Values

Manage Yourself and Others

Engendering Mutual Respect

The Art of Mastery

Set Standards

Create a Participatory Environment

Achieve Constructive Goals

Unlock Ability

A second flip chart contained these words:

Ability	Mastery
Standards	Constructive Goals
Manage	Participatory
Creative Climate	Mutual Respect
Self-motivated	Values

Each of the items on the flip chart, Mike explained, referred to one of the strategies that would be explored during the talk. Mike explained that *breaking out of the box* is a metaphor for successful creative thinking that causes breakthroughs—discoveries that dramatically improve the quality of our lives—in solving problems, developing new products and finding unique solutions to challenges. It utilizes the exercise of connecting nine dots laid out in the form of a box, using only four straight lines without lifting your pen. When we solve problems in unexpected ways, we break out of the box.

The 10 strategies on the flip chart, Mike explained, are the resources, tools, methods and techniques for breaking out of the box, which is accomplished by "connecting the dots" through breakout thinking. Each of the dots represents one of the tools at your disposal for breaking out.

Breakout thinking, Mike explained, is the *ability* to establish *standards* and *manage* a *creative climate* where people are *self-motivated* toward the *mastery* of long-term *constructive goals* in a *participatory environment* of *mutual respect*, compatible with personal *values*.

Mike went on to discuss how to achieve breakthroughs. He emphasized that people must identify how things really are before they take action.

Diane stayed for the entire seminar. Later, she used the concepts Mike outlined and found them to be valuable tools for improving her own performance and for business achievement. Soon after the seminar, she and Mike began working together, collaborating on a number of projects. Their sense of mission and desire to share their findings about creativity led to the formation of the Creative Thinking Association of America, of which Diane is now president. She has worked with Mike for more than 10 years, helping to provide companies with unique processes and designs that are changing the way people think and work. Together, they supply resources for creative work environments, increased productivity and innovative project development. Together, they wrote the forerunner to this book, *Think Out of the Box*.

Much of what appears in the following pages may be controversial, but the principles and practices of the people who use breakout thinking have proven over time to lead to success. To help *you* implement these principles and practices, a "Breakthrough Techniques" checklist—listing specific ways to apply what you learned—is provided at the end of each chapter. The more you learn about these techniques, the more you'll be able to achieve when applying them.

Why break out of the box?

One goal of every life form is, at least in part, to get out of the box—to experience the kinds of breakthroughs that lead to complete fulfillment. Salmon, for example, have adapted the unique ability to swim upstream each spring to spawn, ensuring the propagation of their species. When we overcome an obstacle by adapting to a new situation, we follow the evolutionary path and act to fulfill our own highest potential. *Effective methods of thinking* are the first step. Using *proven concepts* to produce breakthroughs is the second step.

Why think out of the box? To live. To be. To create. To renew. Why break out of the box? To revive. To innovate. To implement. To fulfill.

Our needs fuel the fire for breakout thinking. When we find ourselves in need, we unlock our ability, call upon our values and create the best possible solution. Necessity is often the mother of invention—but it is ultimately drive, will and determination that deliver the goods.

What if Henry Ford had said, "What's wrong with the horse and buggy?"
What if Michelangelo had said, "I don't do ceilings"?
What if Thomas Edison had said, "Candles are fine"?

We also break out of the box to gain competitive superiority in our ventures in the global community. The world desperately needs breakthrough solutions to an endless list of problems and social issues. Despite all of our technology, despite all of our modern conveniences, despite all of our scientific advances, the world awaits a new kind of leadership—leadership that offers breakout approaches and innovative thinking rather than the usual pedestrian quick fixes or short-term "corrections" that do damage in the long run.

Because of their complexity, today's challenges defy a quick fix! Instead, they require a comprehensive new philosophy of management, leadership and personal living that is apolitical and devoted to finding breakthroughs that are constructive for everyone.

Walt Disney used to say, "Think beyond your lifetime if you want to accomplish something truly worthwhile. Put together a 50-year master plan. Thinking 50 years ahead forces you to engage in a quality of thinking that will also improve your present thinking."

Walt's brother Roy once said, "You get a good 'bottom line' by doing good 'top-line' thinking. Top-line thinking gets at the causes that create your bottom-line effects." Today, we need more "top-liners." "Top-line" thinking helps us to break out of the box to produce better bottom lines.

As part of their teaching, design and project work, Mike and Diane hear the same desires again and again from the people they work with: "We need a totally new solution—a breakthrough." On a global level, our survival will depend on a revival, a revival of solid thinking rather than superficial thinking.

Buckminster Fuller, the inventor of the geodesic dome, captured the issue perfectly. "The world's term paper is due," he said. "We've done enough research and read enough books. We've studied for centuries. Now it's time to write. God wants the paper turned in now."

Profiles of breakout thinkers

Role models are the best teachers, because they make ideas real and measurable rather than hypothetical. After each of the 10 chapters of this book is a profile of an outstanding breakout thinker, a superlative person who successfully illustrates the principles discussed in *Break Out of the Box*:

- ◆ E. Cardon Walker (retired chief executive officer of the Walt Disney Company).
- ◆ Mae Carden (teacher; founder, the Carden Schools).
- ◆ J. Willard Marriott (founder, the Marriott Corporation; philanthropist).
- ◆ Walt and Roy Disney (filmmakers; founders, the Walt Disney Company).
- ◆ Val J. Halamandaris (author; publisher; founder and chief executive officer, National Association for HomeCare).
- ◆ Jack Nicklaus (golfer; businessman).
- ◆ Dr. Roy A. Burkhart (minister; author; founder, the Community Church of America).
- ◆ Dr. Albert Suthers (missionary; professor, Ohio Wesleyan University).

♦ Dr. Hugh Missledine (psychiatrist; author).

♦ Louis Lundborg (retired chairman of the board, the Bank of America).

Ten profiles. Ten thinkers. Ten people who understood how to break out of the box.

Our world will always need out-of-the-box thinkers and leaders—people like Andrew Carnegie, who said, "Take everything from me and leave me my people. I'll rebuild."

Where are you, Andrew Carnegie?

Who will help us move beyond our outmoded, slow and corrupt public practices and actually *cut* government expenditures? Who will revive the idea that serving your country is not a lucrative career choice, but an obligation? Where is the politician who loves and understands science, architecture, philosophy, business and the arts?

Come back, Thomas Jefferson!

Who will show us how to make education exciting and relevant again by breaking up the academic bureaucracy?

Revisit us, Aristotle! Revisit us, Plato!

Who will teach us how to have fulfilling, meaningful and happy lives? Who will teach us harmony, inner peace and love once again?

Speak to us again, St. Francis, Helen Keller and Dr. Norman Vincent Peale!

Buckminster Fuller said, "We humans were designed for complete success. All we need is a revival." The revival will depend on our own resoluteness to *break out of the box*. The ideas presented in this book will help you meet the challenges you face by going beyond conventional responses to reach higher creativity...and this is what stimulates *breakthroughs*!

How to Catch the Big One

"To have begun is to have done half the task. Dare to be wise."
—Horace, Roman poet and satirist, 65-8 B.C.

We* want to help you catch the big one—the trophy fish.

This "fish" is the *breakout idea* or *new approach* that will help you take strategic advantage of your own unique talent and potential. The question is: How do you catch a trophy fish?

Most fishermen know about the trick of fishing "in the hatch"—the hatch being the spot where new insects swarm together above the surface of the water, having just emerged from the larva stage. Because many fish aggressively swim up to the surface and try to nab those insects, fishermen often drop camouflaged, hook-bearing "insects" onto the surface of the water and let them float there, hoping to hook their prey. It's a common practice...that sometimes results in common fish on the line.

But what if you want an *uncommon* fish? One you can mount on your wall and tell some stories about? One that really illustrates your fishing prowess?

The *expert* fishermen know techniques that the others don't know. They know that to catch the big fish, you don't fish right *in* the hatch. Instead, you fish *under* it. The really big fish are at the *bottom,* searching out those juicy morsels, the unhatched larva. Consequently, you want to use a *weighted* lure

---

* As a general rule, the "we" voice in this book refers to us—Mike and Diane—as coauthors. Occasionally, one or the other of us is the topic of a particular story, anecdote or observation. In these cases, we refer to ourselves by our own first names.

that sinks below the surface, or a wet fly instead of a dry fly. That's how you catch the *really* big fish, the trophy-sized specimens that you can boast about.

This practice is the opposite of what everyone else does. If you want to catch the trophy fish, you have to be willing to do something other than follow the crowd. This book will give you the tools to take a more unorthodox approach. It will allow you to fish under the hatch. Think of us as your charter captains. We'll take you fishing...and help you land a "big one" you can hang on your wall. That translates to having a breakthrough and enjoying a real revival of spirit and creativity. (Later in the book, we'll help you create your own "lake" in which to go fishing. This is a metaphor we use for a concept known as a Team Center.)

We're on the lookout for the big one—the breakthrough that produces a surge of adrenaline and a revival of spirit!

We believe that it's the *breakthrough* ideas that lead to personal and organizational revival! This book outlines 10 basic strategies for breaking out of the box. We'd like to give you a preview of these ideas now, to give you a feel for the "lay of the land" you're about to travel. The following brief descriptions offer a sense of how the 10 strategies fit together. Later, we'll go into detail regarding each of the 10 steps.

Step 1: Unlock your ability. Ability is the capacity to get things done. What frees people's ability? How do they unlock it in different situations? What stands in the way of their doing so? How do you stay focused on your ability and avoid diverting your energy? How do you find the best way to implement your ideas?

Step 2: Set standards. Standards serve as models for specific, narrowly defined situations. They are a reflection of values, which are discussed in step 10. A standard enables a value to be translated into a goal. Standards are essential! They are guideposts, channel-markers on the way to achievement. In the absence of standards, one usually finds an absence of achievement.

Step 3: Manage yourself and others. The old definition of management was the ability to get work done through people. Today, management in our boundaryless culture is the ability to help people develop themselves and encourage them to reach their highest potential through work *while having fun*. It's not about the control of people, but rather the *release* of human potential through facilitating cooperation.

Step 4: Establish a creative climate. This means developing a work atmosphere that encourages and stimulates creativity, with a special emphasis on implementing that atmosphere and keeping it running. We will show you how to establish a working atmosphere that fosters high achievement. How can you maintain this climate in your work and personal life on a continuous basis?

Step 5: Understand self-motivation. All human beings, regardless of rank or title, are motivated to act on their own overriding need level. They are also motivated by sex, passion and desire. How can you understand these deep motivating drives and use them constructively?

Step 6: Pursue the art of mastery. How do you become a master? What are the characteristics of mastery? Mediocre, average performance plagues so many areas of society. People need to revive excellence by teaching the principles of mastery over the natural tendency to indulge in lazy or mediocre thinking.

Step 7: Achieve long-term constructive goals. Achievable goals—the doable ones—should be the byproducts of your values and should represent all of your desired end results. How do you achieve these goals with the highest degree of productivity?

Step 8: Create a participatory environment. People usually overlook the opportunities for participation and involvement that the environment itself presents. How does the physical structure with which you surround yourself affect output? How do you design creative environments, ones that encourage rather than discourage spontaneous participation among the people who are working in them?

Step 9: Cultivate mutual respect in dealing with others. Mutual respect is the glue that makes relationships stick together. Mutual respect means having high or special regard for a person who shows that same regard for you. How can you engender that respect? Unfortunately, this critical ingredient for breaking out of the box is often brushed aside without a thought. In place of true respect, you usually find bromides and clichés. What people need is a proven method that fosters the development of mutual respect among team members.

Step 10: Tune up your values. Values are the ideas and beliefs people hold to be important, the underlying principles that determine their actions. How can you understand them and use them to promote fulfillment in your business life and personal life?

Three important human truths to keep in mind

Three important facts about people guide the thinking you will encounter in this book:

First, everyone hurts at some time. The nature of the human condition is such that suffering is, to some degree, a permanent part of everyone's existence. It's part of being mortal. Consequently, we believe a system for personal and organizational breakthroughs must incorporate compassion and understanding as essential features. Such a system helps to reduce hostile interrelationships and lower tension levels through empathy and mutual respect. We incorporate this idea throughout the book.

Second, everyone has longings. Everyone longs to achieve, to be something, to emerge as anything other than a number found on a computer printout. Everyone wants to reach for the stars in a unique way. Wouldn't it be magnificent to use unique strengths and aptitudes to fulfill secret longings, to turn latent dreams into reality? Together, we'll uncover breakout principles that can help satisfy those longings.

Third, everyone requires better skills and more opportunities. Walt Disney once told Mike, "Most people have or cause problems because they lack the skills or the opportunities to be successful in the environments in which they find themselves." Once you've identified the types of professional and people-related skills you need to develop, and once you understand the opportunities you should be taking advantage of, you'll be in a position to excel in today's economy—the economy of the highly trained, technically skilled knowledge worker. We'll help you identify the gaps that you may have—the skills and opportunities you may lack. And *everyone* has gaps of one kind or another.

By reading *Break Out of the Box*, you are taking the critical step of committing to *ongoing* breakthroughs in your learning and development. This is one of the chief attributes of a living, contributing team member: the willingness to learn.

No zombies

You've probably noticed that there are large numbers of people in the world who have graduated from the ranks of the walking *wounded* to the ranks of the walking *dead*. Their eyes glaze over and their minds shut down at the prospect of anything remotely resembling a new approach; they seem to repeat old habits instinctively, regardless of the situation facing them; and they fail to notice when they stumble upon an opportunity.

These are the dead people, the zombies. Who wants to be one of them?

It's tragic to be a zombie shut inside a self-imposed coffin. The world needs living, breathing people who can break down the walls of conformity and mediocrity. That need has motivated us to find ways to break out of the box. Therefore, we emphasize possibilities and propose approaches with a confidence that is based on the success we have experienced *firsthand* in helping people find breakthroughs and what is truly alive within themselves. This confidence is not meant to suggest that we think we have all the answers. We discover new concepts every single day, just as you do, and we revise our thinking accordingly.

We don't believe we have all the answers, and we don't believe in magic formulas, either. Life is a process, one that incorporates trial and error as a prerequisite for success. Those who intimate that there's a single big idea or magic formula you can implement *immediately* do people a disservice.

We don't mean for you to take what follows as strict dogma. Our suggestions are meant as potential eye-openers, door-openers, *box-breakers* for you to implement while using your own unique talents. The ideas in *Break Out of the Box* will help you to come to your own conclusions.

Summary

➤ This book is designed to help you catch the "trophy fish"—the breakthrough idea or new approach that will help you take strategic advantage of your own unique talents and potential.

➤ Catching the big fish often means doing the opposite of what everyone else does.

➤ The chapters that follow offer 10 ideas to help you break out of the box.

➤ Three important facts about people guide the thinking you will encounter in this book: Everyone hurts sometimes, everyone longs for something and everyone requires better skills and more opportunities.

➤ The world needs living, breathing people—not zombies—to break down the walls of conformity and mediocrity. The ideas in this book can help anyone build the foundation necessary to become an "out-of-the-box" thinker.

BREAKTHROUGH CHECKLIST

NEEDS FOR BREAKTHROUGHS	GOALS FOR BREAKTHROUGHS	RESOURCES FOR BREAKTHROUGHS
☑ Products	☑ Invent	☑ An inspirational speech
☑ Services	☑ Create	☑ A big budget
☑ Politics	☑ Discover	☑ A Charrette
☑ Values	☑ Resolve	☑ An effective facilitator
☑ Passion	☑ Redirect	☑ Creative Thinking Techniques
☑ Fulfillment	☑ Reinvigorate	☑ Exercise
☑ Differentiators	☑ Refresh	☑ A creative environment
☑ Happiness	☑ Renew	☑ A good night's sleep
☑ Loyalty	☑ Rejoice	☑ A rally
☑ Forgiveness	☑ Restore	☑ A deep breath
☑ Fun	☑ Revitalize	☑ A massage
☑ Solutions	☑ Reactivate	☑ A listen to your favorite song
☑ Diets	☑ Repair	☑ A good movie
☑ Inspiration	☑ Rejuvenate	☑ A stimulating seminar
☑ Education	☑ Recondition	☑ Expertise
☑ Humor	☑ Reinvent	☑ A good book
☑ Love	☑ Reengineer	☑ A vacation
☑ Peace	☑ Relax	☑ Cueing devices
☑ Health	☑ Reproduce	
	☑ Replenish	
	☑ Revamp	
	☑ Replant	
	☑ Recharge	

CHAPTER 1

Unlocking Your Ability

"Natural abilities are like natural plants, that need pruning by study..."
—Francis Bacon, English philosopher
and essayist, 1561-1626

How do we unlock our abilities? This innocent question is at the heart of a struggle that's been going on since the dawn of human history. What influences someone to achieve his or her maximum potential? Is it the environment? Is it heredity, one's familial predispositions? Is it a combination of the two? If so, which element has the greater influence? Or is it some other factor that remains hidden from our understanding?

We aren't going to try to resolve these vexing questions, but we would like to point out that people who grow up in a deprived environment can succeed at a very high level and find significant personal happiness. It's also true, of course, that there are people from apparently supportive, nurturing environments, environments that offer every imaginable advantage, who have met with extraordinary internal problems, never reaching what might be considered to be the full potential of their abilities. The same statements can be made about hereditary influence. Large numbers of people have been cursed with poor health or other inherited disabilities and have transcended their limitations to lead fulfilling, rich lives marked by surprising achievement. Conversely, people with good looks, perfect health and other apparent genetic advantages often lead desperately *unhappy* lives.

We ask: What is the secret to unlocking one's true potential? And how do we get beyond bromides in answering this elusive question?

We are neither geneticists nor behavioral scientists, but we believe there is a critical factor in personal achievement and fulfillment that is influenced by both heredity and environment: the phenomenon of nonthinking.

What *is* nonthinking? It's reacting before we think, before evaluating the reality before us. This practice stops growth, stops breakthroughs, stops *every-thing*. It is inherently *deadening*, choking off the development of natural ability, because it causes denial of the way things really are. Nonthinking creates a zombie mentality. The practice of nonthinking may very well, more than any other single factor, compromise the objective of unlocking one's true potential. Fortunately, however, the degree to which we become nonthinkers is not beyond our control. We *can* change our behavior.

Nonthinking has three major causes.

The first major cause of nonthinking: ignoring our past

If we want to unlock our ability, we must resolve to stop ignoring the past and what it has done to us. We must *understand*, rather than deny, our past experiences if we hope to make a realistic assessment of our current prejudices and predispositions.

Mike once worked with a woman by the name of Gail. She once asked him, rather enviously, "Are you *always* up?" The question surprised him. He explained that, no, he very often encountered problems that got him down.

"But you always *seem* up," Gail persisted. "How do you do it?"

Mike told her this story: "I was born in the small town of Greenville, Ohio. My grandfather was a grocer; so was my father. We lived next door to a dear, old, white-haired man named Adam Erhardt, who regularly gave me glasses of home-brewed dandelion wine as I walked past his house on the way to kindergarten. (The teachers couldn't figure out why I kept falling asleep once I made it to school!) Adam Erhardt contributed significantly to my enjoyment of my time in kindergarten. He was a genial, happy, white-bearded fellow whom I believed, for some time, to be God.

"One day I went over to his house to show him one of my creations—a collection of people I had made from empty spools of thread and pipe cleaners and whom I kept in shoeboxes. Shoebox people, I called them. I shared with Adam my make-believe conversations with the shoebox people, and I passed along their many observations on life. He took a deep interest in my creations, just as he took a deep interest in me. A day or so later, in the evening, I was preparing for bed, and I heard a knock at the door. It was Adam, who started a conversation with my mother, Virginia, a conversation I overheard from the top of the stairs.

"Adam said to her, 'Virginia, you should be very proud; that boy of yours is always going to be creative.' He told her about the shoebox people, and I drank in every word of it."

After he'd shared this story with Gail, Mike said, "Gail, what I heard from the top of the stairs is what I believed about myself all through my childhood and early life. Now, the question is, what did *you* hear at the top of *your* stairs?"

"I heard just the opposite," Gail said slowly. "I always heard my parents talk about how frail, sickly and gawky I was. That I was fragile, that I always seemed to have a sensitive stomach, that I was always going to be a pain in the neck."

Those were the messages Gail received from the top of the stairs—and sure enough, those realities of her childhood experience manifested themselves in her adult life. Mike's question helped Gail take the first step in recognizing the true nature of her past experiences. He helped her to stop ignoring her own history, which was clouding her thinking in the present and was, perhaps, the reason she regarded "always being up" as so difficult an achievement.

Recognizing that early messages have an impact is the first step to *overcoming* the problem—and beginning to think, rather than simply repeating old patterns we learned from childhood. This may seem like a basic observation, but it is fundamental to the process of gaining insight.

Gail's story is one Mike tells often during his seminars. Once, in La Jolla, California, he was relaxing around the swimming pool with a very prominent man who had heard Gail's story that day during the program. He and Mike were quietly watching the sunset when the man put his arm around Mike and asked if he could relate his own childhood experience. Mike noticed that tears were in his eyes.

"What's the matter?" Mike asked.

"That story about Gail and the shoebox," the man explained after he composed himself, "made quite an impression on me. Mike, when I was growing up, I, too, heard just the opposite from what you heard at the top of the stairs. Once, my father picked me up and put me on the mantel, then told me to jump. When I did, he stepped away. I fell onto the hearth. I remember seeing my own blood from the blow I took when I fell. I cried and cried. My father told me, 'Son, I want you to know that you can't trust anybody in this world—starting with your own father.' "

Mike is fairly certain he must have been the first person with whom this gentleman ever shared that story. He also feels certain that this man's revisiting that traumatic event was a major factor in his learning to look at himself and the world more accurately, more incisively and more realistically...a *breakthrough*!

How many snap judgments—such as never being able to trust people—do we make because we don't review events from our past? We can't casually dismiss our own prejudices if we hope to break out of the box and leave the nonthinking mode. We have to accept our prejudices for what they are and act on the best, new, solid information we can gather for ourselves.

Buckminster Fuller said, "One of the things you have to do in order to remember where you came from is ride on your hobbyhorse." That's a strange remark to make, but Fuller would, from time to time, *literally* ride the same hobbyhorse he had enjoyed as a child. By doing this as an adult, he was able to remember his childhood experiences and keep his perspective clear.

Ride your own hobbyhorse now and then. Don't ignore your past or pretend you've resolved every issue arising out of it. You haven't. None of us has.

If Buckminster Fuller could gain a better perspective from riding his hobbyhorse, we can gain a better perspective from riding ours! Do some thinking about the events of your past and their many ramifications, and do it as soon as possible. The sooner you do, the sooner you'll start moving toward a point of view that reflects things the way they are, rather than the way you've been told they are, or the way you want them to be. Which brings us to...

The second major cause of nonthinking: choosing *wishful* thinking

Wishful thinking turns people into nonthinkers. "I wish my life were more orderly," "I wish I had more leisure time," "I wish I were doing better at my job," "I wish my relationship with my spouse were better"—all of these formulations (and their many variations) delude people into focusing attention on what they wish were taking place, rather than what actually is. Wishful thinking is actually a form of *non*thinking.

Walt Disney once said to Mike, "The saddest thing in the world must be when someone who is about to die is thinking, 'What could I have done, what might I have been, if I had *acted* instead of merely *wishing*?' "

Our seminar and consulting work allows us to address a wide variety of audiences. Once, Mike was giving a program at a prison, and he conducted a one-on-one session with a man who was in solitary confinement. This man was a multiple murderer. Throughout his meeting with Mike, he insisted, quite lucidly, that he was actually the Messiah. Talk about wishful thinking!

Delusional wishful thinking is not always evil, however. It's human nature to drop the following superficial bromides over reality: "Everything's going to work out," "What you need is to be positive," "No problem."

In our book *Think Out of the Box*, we talked about the importance of clarifying the concept of positive thinking so that it's not a distortion of reality— saying you don't have something you do, or saying you do have something you don't. "I can deny the reality of this disease, I don't feel this symptom, I don't really need to accept this," wishful thinking says. In that way, wishful thinking can be more than just dangerous—it can be deadly.

True positive thinking is realistic—it accepts facts, rather than attempting to whitewash them. Athletes who must visualize a successful run down a treacherous ski slope don't imagine that the slope is laid out in a straight line. They envision correct turns through each and every one of the curves, exactly as they will face them during the actual run.

Wishful thinking in the business world also carries hollow and ultimately menacing promises: "The turnaround is coming," "The problem is you don't really believe in what you're doing," "You just have to stay positive," "If you hang in there, things are going to be different."

When we cautiously wait for conditions to become the way we want them to be rather than taking specific action based on the facts, we usually find that we must settle in for a very long wait indeed. We may even find that we have doomed ourselves to repeat the past again.

Wishful thinking is the *poverty* of thinking. And we can't afford to go broke on wishful thinking if we're ever to know the luxury of *clear* thinking.

The third major cause of nonthinking: being critical instead of analytical

It's often easier to criticize than to create. It's easier to blame than to find solutions. It's easier to focus our attentions on who's at fault than to work with others to find the best ways to proceed. These approaches may be easier, but are any of them *thinking*?

Rather than casting aspersions on people's behavior, we should dedicate ourselves to *uncovering the root cause of the problem.* Once we've taken this step, people are open to learning. We can help them grow through training and coaching.

There's a catch to this approach, though. Unlike assigning blame, being analytical (instead of critical) requires thinking.

We face complex problems in a world of constantly expanding technology. In business today, there seems to be a constant attempt to boil things down to a few simple points, rather than to engage in rigorous thinking to uncover the true cause of problems. Some theoreticians argue that we can manage a business—or take control of our careers, or train someone in a complex new procedure—in a minute. Lee Iacocca didn't turn Chrysler around in a minute. We shouldn't expect to get quick resolutions of every crisis we face, either. We can't, because one-minute solutions are often not solutions at all. They represent wishful thinking, which is not analytical thinking.

We have to take the time to analyze the situation before us, even if that means committing ourselves to pursuing the task of studying the situation carefully. This is certainly true of child-rearing, and it's true of business, too. Analyzing—rather than criticizing—is a necessary prerequisite to unlocking ability and resolving problems.

Your personal breakthrough, just as for a child who's learning to spell or a colleague who's learning how to coordinate a difficult project, requires both quality and quantity time.

Unlocking ability may mean challenging the status quo

Once we unleash our ability by freeing ourselves from *nonthinking* and committing ourselves to observant, *analytical thinking,* we may find ourselves in a position to challenge some cherished assumptions. Challenge them!

Suppose we conclude, after a careful assessment of the facts, that our company is following a dead-end street. Suppose we're wondering whether we should consider a radical departure from the line of business we typically pursue. Follow that path through! Look at the options! Don't assume that you have to keep doing what you've been doing all these years. The basic business of many corporations we work with is not the core business they started with initially. It may be the same way with your business.

Four stages of ability

Abandoning a nonthinking mind-set means understanding that, in any given area, we are working at one of four stages of ability:

1. Ignorance (not to be confused with stupidity).

2. Awareness.

3. Knowledge.

4. Wisdom.

Ignorance, the first stage, is simply unrealized potential. Many people make the mistake of believing that those who have not yet achieved their full potential are unintelligent by nature. We don't believe there are many stupid people in the world. Instead, we believe that there are many people who haven't had the opportunity to develop themselves.

This is one reason why it doesn't make sense to talk down to people. Treating people as though they're stupid only breeds enmity. Being condescending to people establishes walls of resistance—and that's not conducive to breakthroughs! Whether we're talking to a truck driver or a banker, our conversational partner may have trouble understanding an unfamiliar word but will probably grasp what we're getting at once it's explained clearly.

It's the same for everyone. When we don't know something, the first step is to admit that we don't know it, and figure out what needs to be done in order to learn it.

What we do is determined by what we are; what we are is determined by what we think; what we think is determined by what we learn; what we learn is determined by what we believe; and what we believe is determined by what we're exposed to and what we do with that exposure.

Some people have not been exposed to very much, but are eager to learn. Some people are exposed to a great deal, but have trained themselves to hold back, to remain cautious. We *can't* hold back if we want to break out of box. We must identify the areas where we need to grow—by becoming sensitive to our own gaps and shortcomings.

Once we've done this, we can move from ignorance (the first level) to awareness (the second level). Then we'll begin to seek knowledge (the third level). We'll begin to learn about the challenges we face, to thirst after facts and to question what's in front of us. Finally, after a determined effort, we'll be in position for the fourth level: wisdom, in which we attain a more profound and philosophical perspective about ourselves and the world in which we live.

Staging Ability

Stage	Causes	Results
I. Ignorance		
• Not knowing that you don't know	A. No exposure	A. Naiveté
• Not stupid	B. No experience	B. Unrealistic thinking
	C. Ignoring things	C. Being talked down to
	D. No training	D. Indifference to growth
II. Awareness		
• Experiencing things	A. Using all five senses	A. Clean beginnings
• Feeling things	B. Continuing to learn	B. Exposure and learning
• Not neurotic	C. Having desire	C. Motivation
III. Knowledge		
• Having resources to meet your needs	A. The right environment, like a Team Center	A. Success in all five equities (see pages 122-124)
	B. Resource-rich environments	B. Achievement
IV. Wisdom		
• Wise beyond your age	A. Practicing, which makes us better (but not perfect)	A. Advancement
• Having accumulated learning with good sense	B. Acceptance of life	B. Meditation
		C. Spiritual development

John Belushi, the comic whose genius was cut short by drug abuse, had a catch phrase he loved to bellow at people: "Wise up!" On the night of Belushi's death, newscaster Dan Rather summed up the comedian's time on earth by reminding America of Belushi's injunction to "wise up!"—and closed the epitaph with this observation: "He never did."

Life is too long not to do it right. That's right—it's too long. Count the number of Monday mornings between birth and death in the average lifespan. Do we really want to go through all those Monday mornings without *wising up*?

We can't learn anything from experiences we're not having. We can't have many valid experiences if we're in a nonthinking mind-set, because nonthinking means tuning out of the situation rather than tuning into it.

Humanity's collective ability to get things done is awesome, but so is its capacity for neglecting facts. The choice is ours. We can unleash our ability in a thousand different ways—overcome disaster, reverse a downward trend, restore peace—but only when we commit to overcoming the obstacles that stand in our way and looking with open eyes at our true situation and our true selves.

The more you are like yourself, the less you are like anyone else.

Summary

➤ Ability is our capacity to accomplish things.

➤ One of the chief obstacles to maximum achievement is what we call *nonthinking*.

➤ The first major cause of nonthinking is ignoring our past. What each of us hears "at the top of the stairs" as a child has a profound influence on our later growth and achievement. In the case of negative early messages, *recognizing* that those messages have had an impact is the first step to *overcoming* that impact.

➤ The second major cause of nonthinking is choosing wishful thinking. Delusional thinking can be dangerous, even deadly, and is not to be confused with constructive positive thinking.

➤ The third major cause of nonthinking is being critical instead of being analytical.

➤ Unlocking ability may mean challenging the status quo.

➢ There are four stages of ability: ignorance, awareness, knowledge and wisdom.

➢ Ignorance is only unrealized potential. When we don't know something, the first step is to admit that we don't know it, and figure out what we need to do to learn it.

➢ What we do is determined by what we are; what we are is determined by what we think; what we think is determined by what we learn; what we learn is determined by what we believe; what we believe is determined by what we're exposed to and what we do with that exposure.

Profile: Unlocked Ability

E. Cardon Walker

Chief Executive Officer (retired), The Walt Disney Company

"Breaking out of the box" comes very close to being a perfect description of Walt Disney's operating philosophy. He was a classic example of a breakthrough thinker. The one man who knows from long personal experience what Walt Disney's soul was like has to be E. Cardon Walker, who rose through the ranks to become president (1971-1976) and CEO (1976-1983) of the Walt Disney Company.

The man who inherited a dream

Walt Disney's legacy, which Walker (who goes by the nickname "Card") tirelessly nurtured and supported, was based on breakthrough thinking. Card had the rare chance to look into the soul of a genius when he worked with Walt. Card possessed the experience, and the personal intelligence, to work at the very highest level of the Disney organization, and to learn the secrets of one of the world's greatest entrepreneurs. He is a competent authority on breakthrough thinking who followed in the steps of the master—a little like the son that Walt Disney never had.

We've discussed ability, the capacity to get things done. This is what Card unleashed at Disney Studios throughout his career there.

He was a high-voltage force, a catalyst for action. He made those who worked for the Disney organization (including Mike) believe in their own capabilities. That's the mark of a true leader.

Card's unbounded enthusiasm for the mission of keeping Walt's dream alive was like glue—it stuck to people! As a leader, Card was sincere, and he appealed to the deepest emotions of his people. They shared his dedication, because they sensed his total commitment. He inspired them to do good work.

Early morning visits

Even before he became President of the Walt Disney Company, Walker was a force to be reckoned with. Nearly every day, he would be in his office at the studio by 6 a.m. He set a clear example for everyone.

Ken Seiling, for decades Disney's personnel director, was walking past Card's office with Mike early one morning. "He's always in there," Ken remarked. "He's always *been* in there. In fact, you can set your watch by him. And he's always available to any of us at any time."

Card was so respected, though, that no one would interrupt his early morning work session with unimportant matters. Usually, just knowing that he was there, ready to help anyone who needed help, was enough. His visible dedication created an atmosphere where breakthroughs occurred because there was deep desire and genuine passion in the atmosphere.

With Card, as with Walt, there were no mysteries about what was necessary for breaking out of the box: hard work, intelligence and the tenacity to never give up until you come to closure.

The word "closure" epitomizes Card's *modus operandi*. He always wanted to see your plan for implementation, and that plan had to be focused on what could be delivered. Nothing was to be left up in the air. No vagueness was allowed.

One of the organizational development teams was working on a proposed Disney ski resort at Mineral King Valley in California. (Mike and Bob Mathieson were the group leaders for a study related to the project.) You can bet that every team member learned how important it was to prepare an effective master plan.

"Pin it down," Card insisted. "Don't be fuzzy about anything. Do your homework. In your minds, walk through the question 'How do we get the Disney touch into this ski resort?' Do that step by step, item by item. We want it to be a family place, where kids aren't left out. Walt believes that we have a unique opportunity to bring something new and different to the world of skiing. Therefore, the old solutions, services and standard features won't be good enough."

He also said, "We've got to do our research and development well enough so that we see what's missing from the ski scene *from the family's point of view*. We want to break out of the conventional mold and make it really exciting for everyone. We don't want muddy or frozen dirt streets. We should have guests ice-skating around the village on specially designed skates. We've got to romance the whole business of skiing! You fellows need to get out of Burbank and go visit some of the best ski resorts in the world. Learn what's up. Learn what's current. Go talk to the guests. Talk to the ski instructors. Visit the restaurants and shops. Ride the lifts. Study the slopes. Take a run down the hill!" His enthusiasm got everyone excited. The whole team was ready to take off immediately!

On that project, Card widened everyone's vision. He challenged the team not to be provincial in their thinking, and he provided each member of the team with an education about how to approach a project from all angles: master planning, research and development, communications, idea generation and (last but not least) how to do a briefing for Walt Disney. Although the project never moved ahead to the implementation stage, the research for it was an unforgettable experience for everyone involved.

Today, Mike is quite certain that every member of an organizational development team who worked on projects under Card's tutelage enjoyed greater career success as a result. No graduate school could have any course that would help students more than Card Walker's "How to Have Breakthroughs 101."

Here's an example of the guidance he offered on that ski project. We think it can be adapted to any situation in which people's abilities need to be tapped to maximum advantage.

Mineral King Ski Project: Preparation and Homework

1. Select a team that can get the job done and work well together. Avoid putting the team together for political reasons or to make points. Consider only the talent and what you want to achieve.

2. Study the ski industry by reading and talking to experts in every phase of the business.

3. Visit the best ski resorts—and some of the worst. Learn from their operations, instructors, guests and support organizations. Ask yourself: How do we build a dynamic culture in Disney Village? What will be the unique factors?

4. Develop a preliminary master plan that includes layout, traffic flow, ideas on handling people, waste management plans, services, staffing requirements, costs and distinct features.

5. Participation and briefing materials should include storyboards that will display our background materials, R&D findings, ideas, models, recommendations, pictures and artwork. We should be able to view the project from start to finish. Do a rehearsal and a run-through, always *before* the briefing. Practice. Never fly by the seat of your pants.

6. Prepare an executive briefing on your preliminary findings and your recommendations.

It's easy to understand why Disney plans were so well-executed when the leader was a person like Card Walker. He and Walt both used to say, "Leave nothing to chance." They meant that, before committing to a project, they wanted to be able to walk around in it. They never wanted to be in the preliminary planning phase while they were executing.

Card will probably never know how profound his influence was on the hundreds of people he trained, people who achieved noteworthy success in their careers because of his superlative leadership and example. Mike feels that his own accomplishments have resulted from exposure to this exceptional man.

News that stunned the world

An unbelievable news flash on a dark day in 1966: Walt Disney was dead. The world wept; nations around the globe lowered their flags to half-mast. Here's how Mike, who was at Disney headquarters when the news came through, remembered the swirl of events at this extraordinary time during a recent discussion.

"I left my office shortly after the announcement, walked down the hallway of the animation building and passed Card, who was running up the steps between floors. Neither of us spoke a word. We just looked at each other and felt the pain together for a moment.

"Bill Walsh, the producer of the megahit *Mary Poppins*, was standing by a window on the third floor, crying profusely. He'd loved Walt so. It was a sad time.

"Our group had been scheduled to have dinner with Card, but that was postponed until the next night, when we gathered at the Smoke House Restaurant in Burbank. I'd spent hundreds of hours there talking about the Disney philosophy over the past seven years.

"The dinners usually began with cocktails and snacks, which allowed time for socializing and informal talk. I decided to go early, about 5 p.m., to check things out and make sure the room was set up properly. Normally, the restaurant and bar were completely empty until half past five, and at that point people from the entertainment industry began to come in for drinks. It was a popular spot; Warner Brothers and NBC were located just across the street.

"One lonely figure was seated at the bar: Card Walker. He appeared to be very dejected. His head was lowered slightly downward toward his glass. A chill went down my spine. I couldn't remember ever seeing my dynamic boss in a posture that showed such sorrow and pain.

"I was hesitant about invading Card's private moment. I assumed that he needed this brief respite before facing the evening ahead, which would no doubt be filled with questions from anxious men who wanted to talk about the future of the Disney organization without Walt Disney. Would there be a future that could compare with what had gone before? That was the question that was on everyone's mind.

"Rick, the Smoke House manager, said, 'There's a friend of yours at the bar, Mike.'

" 'Yes, I see him,' I replied.

"I didn't speak, but instead just sat down beside Card on the next stool. Neither of us said anything for several very long moments. My heart was pounding. The emotions were running strong.

"Finally, Card said, 'We've been here under better circumstances, Mike.' Then there was another silence. Card took a drink and went on: 'I can't believe he's gone. He was such a wonderful guy with such a big dream. We'll just have to get through this somehow.'

"I stared straight ahead for a moment. 'Would you rather cancel this dinner tonight, Card?' I asked. 'Everyone will understand.'

"Card shook his head. 'No,' he said. 'I think not. We've got to go on and make his dream come true. It's just so hard to do.'

"Another long silence followed; I was pretty choked up and wasn't up for much more talking. I put my hand on Card's shoulder as a gesture of understanding. At that moment, another member of the group arrived and I went over to greet him, leaving Card to himself for a while.

"That night, the personnel at the Smoke House, including Rick, the manager, knew how despondent we all were over Walt. They were especially helpful on this night. They went out of their way to serve us a delicious meal, offered us excellent service and showed some welcome kindness to a group of very downbeat men.

"The discussion followed the dinner, and Card was in top form. I found it difficult to believe that this was the same man who had been so distraught just a little while earlier. I took notes at what turned out to be a historic get-together.

"Here's what Card said: 'What do we do now that Walt's gone? We've got to make his dream for Florida come true. You fellows right here will be part of the team that makes it happen, just as he envisioned it. And we've got to pull together as never before. Fellows, Walt wanted to build a model city down in Florida where people could live a quality of life that they couldn't find anywhere else. We have to find a way to make that dream happen.

" 'The world needs a good example to follow, a prototype. That's where we came up with the working title, EPCOT. It stands for Experimental Prototype City of Tomorrow. But it's just a working title. It will always be in a state of becoming. It will never be finished. It will always be a place for experimenting, for trying out new ideas. It will serve as a showcase for what can and will be in tomorrow's world. Imagine a place...'

"Card paused and choked up.

" 'It's a shame he had to die. I just don't understand some things at all.

" 'Please excuse me, my feelings sort of overtook me for a moment.' Then Card continued, 'Imagine a place where you move around without fear of being hit by a speeding car. Instead, we'd have people movers, monorails, boats and special bicycle paths. It would be wonderful. Imagine a place where there are no garbage bags sitting out in the streets twice a week. Instead, we'd take care of the waste with advanced technology. Imagine a place where schools use the finest tools known to man for the purpose of educating our children to fulfill their dreams. We'd have a Walt Disney Institute or University down there. Imagine a place where culture, recreation, theater, music, theme shops and sports are available to you, no more than a stone's throw away. Imagine having an advanced university where the world's greatest teachers come, and hospitals employ the finest doctors and use the very latest procedures. Imagine an airport of the future, showcase industrial parks for business, maybe a motion picture studio. Imagine all of this, and even more—things we haven't even thought of yet. Imagine it!'

"He stopped talking, and we all felt that old magic, that sense that anything was possible. We all wanted to make this dream come true. Card had unlocked our ability, our capacity to get things done. We felt strengthened because he had painted a picture for us, a picture that reflected Walt's fantastic vision. Card had converted us into zealots. He'd reminded us that we were part of something big. He gave us a purpose, a reason to work like hell and forget about everything else.

"A young finance guy in that group got so worked up in that tiny gabled room that he could hardly contain his enthusiasm! Card had shared with us a very special kind of motivation, the kind that makes ordinary people extraordinary, the kind, I think, that is missing too often in the affairs of people."

At that meeting at the Smoke House Restaurant, Mike saw the spirit that would guide the next phase of the Disney organization when he looked in Card Walker's eyes. He saw the *breakthrough* philosopher, the man who taps the full ability of all he encounters. It was a moment Mike will never forget. He saw a team that began the process of breaking out of the box that night and tapping its full abilities. EPCOT and Walt Disney World are now a reality in Florida, bringing happiness and education to millions of people every year.

How many men like Card Walker can we expect to encounter to help us tap our abilities for such massive undertakings? Sadly, not enough. But we can start on our own. We all possess a special kind of motivation, the kind that's necessary to climb our dreams, scale them, tame them. We can all be committed to summoning the best within ourselves to turn those dreams into reality. When we do, we'll be following

Card Walker's example, the example of a magnificent leader who kept Walt Disney's dream alive by *unlocking the abilities of others*.

E. Cardon Walker's Breakout Qualities

- ◆ Inspiring
- ◆ Motivational
- ◆ Dynamic
- ◆ Humble
- ◆ Highly intelligent
- ◆ Action-oriented
- ◆ Willing to offer opportunity
- ◆ Involved
- ◆ Passionate

BREAKTHROUGH TECHNIQUES

GETTING THINGS ACCOMPLISHED

☑ The person in charge should select team leader(s) and assign the task. Is the task clear? Is the goal clear?

☑ The team leader, then, should select core team members. Make sure the team members selected know something about the project. Have you selected the right team members? Are they excited about the challenge?

☑ Collaborate with those who can contribute strength to your project. Who are they?

☑ Learn and study the knowledge that is available through academic resources. What is the body of knowledge? Where is it located? Who is the contact?

☑ Consult with known experts and authorities in applicable fields of specialty. Who are they? Have they been engaged?

☑ List the items and issues that must be brought to closure. Get agreement on them. Who is responsible for checking progress? Schedule briefings with sanctioners.

☑ Do you have people with the skills and know-how to implement your plan or strategy? List them by name. Have they allocated the required amount of time to implement the plan? Have appropriate resources been allocated?

CHAPTER 2

Setting Standards

"How far that little candle throws his beams!"
—William Shakespeare

The ability to break out of the box depends on the ability to set appropriate standards. This is not the same as blindly following "rules" without regard to the outcomes of your efforts. Rules are the guidelines you develop in order to fulfill your standards.

What *are* standards? They are guiding principles governing specific situations, principles that should not be ignored except in truly extraordinary circumstances. Here are four important guidelines that will help you establish, re-establish or get back in touch with your standards.

Guideline #1: Standards are reflections of values.

We'll explain values at a deeper level later on. For now, let's simply say that standards provide specific, practical examples of what we want to accomplish. These principles serve as guideposts for progress toward larger, more expansive objectives—objectives that are rooted in who you are and what you consider to be important.

Here's an illustration to help you understand the relationship between values and standards: Suppose there's a successful company operating a chain of amusement parks whose singular internal value can best be summed up in this way: "We really care for people." That's the value this company embraces wholeheartedly, the value that helps to distinguish it from others. It's a good idea for the company to place a written statement of this value on a sign posted in a place where everyone can see it, but is that enough? How does it make the idea of "really caring for people" tangible? A specific standard should grow out of that guiding philosophy.

Let's assume that this amusement park features a high-speed roller coaster, one that's designed to look and feel like a rocket ship. At a company that doesn't actually follow through on its stated value, the idea of "really caring for people" might be expressed in a "secular" form—through hiring an advertising agency to develop a campaign around the idea of caring for people, but then not working with the employees to develop a plan for action that is really based on the idea. At the company we have in mind, though, the rocket ship ride exemplifies the core value from top to bottom. How? By people working together to implement the most ingenious, state-of-the-art safety features imaginable on the roller coaster.

Throughout the ride, a complex system of electronic sensors control the brakes (which are embedded in the tracks). The system is checked rigorously and on an ongoing basis by technicians who personally monitor the system as a backup. The coasters themselves are timed and checked every single day, and the distance between various coasters is carefully computed for maximum safety in the dispatch interval.

Can you think of a better way to "care for people" than to take the time, commit to the expense and make the effort to ensure the ride is as safe as modern technology and advanced operational creativity can make it? The standard reflects the value! The value? "We care for people." The standard? "Nothing less than the most comprehensive safety standards imaginable will do."

In another organization, the underlying core value might be this one: "We want to provide state-of-the-art products." How would this value be implemented? By allowing employees to innovate. By taking action to make the old obsolete. By committing to never shoving old merchandise off the shelf and into consumers' hands in order to get rid of it. Is such an approach expensive? Sometimes. Is it in keeping with the company's underlying value? Yes. And it is only by taking concrete action to fulfill this value—only by setting complementary standards—that the value will pay off in the long run in terms of what matters most: a great reputation.

Guideline #2: Leadership without set standards has little or no effect.

If you're working with others, you must be able to appeal to mutually acceptable, mutually understood standards. If you're working independently, the demands of discipline in "self-leadership" make definitive standards just as important: You need standards to help keep your own efforts on track!

Leadership without set standards is not effective leadership. If people don't have a cognitive understanding of the standards they're supposed to uphold—or if the standards are vague, hard to figure out or inconsistently applied—leadership has little or no effect.

It's a good practice to write down your standards. But try not to become hung up on terminology. One company calls these guideposts "traditions," and this gets the job done just as effectively as calling them "standards."

Whatever you call them, write down the standards that you and others will act to uphold. Write down what you want your employees to commit to. Write it down in a way that everyone will understand. Make it specific and consistent with your values. Better yet, have employees create the standards. This will help build commitment. (See Chapter 10 for a full discussion of values and their impact upon work.)

Standards should be both concise and comprehensive. Before hiring anyone, one hotel chain makes sure that the following standard has been read and agreed to: "We believe that people have a right to their personal property and the things they possess. That includes the people who work with us and the people who visit with us. Therefore, it is our philosophy not to take things from each other or the people who stay with us."

What a fantastic standard! And what results it has delivered! This chain of hotels has one of the lowest rates of employee theft in the industry.

Leadership—of yourself or others—sets standards for performance. This kind of leadership is not vague. It makes people want to follow the principles that have been laid out—or find another company to work for if they can't uphold the standards.

There have been a few people who have interviewed at the hotel chain we just mentioned who decided, after reading the "personal property" standard, to walk away and withdraw their application for the job! They didn't want to uphold the company's standard. By making important standards perfectly clear, you win buy-in from team members who are inspired by these standards and, frequently, avoid wasting time and energy on people who aren't.

Ask for commitment! Explain the standards to people, and most of the time they'll realize on their own when they've gone over the line. (For that matter, you'll realize when you've gone over the line, too, which contributes to self-discipline.)

Are you a parent? Clearly established standards work just as well at home as they do on the job. And just as they do at work, the standards will change over time as circumstances change and values shift. At Mike's house, there was a standard in place for his son Johnny when he was little: *Don't hit Vanessa even when you think she deserves it.* By enunciating and discussing the "no-hitting" standard with his son, Mike was able to make it work—not 100 percent of the time, but enough of the time to bring about a big improvement.

There was another standard in the house: *No one will eat goldfish from the goldfish pond.* (We develop standards to meet pressing contingencies, right?) Once, after having reached agreement on that standard, Mike came across his son holding half of a goldfish. Let's face it: Young children are tricky and you have to keep your eye on them to make sure standards are being observed. But listen to what happened next! Mike asked him, "Where's the other half of that goldfish?" There was a pause, and then the little boy pointed to his stomach. After this piece of self-incrimination, he put himself in the chair for a time out!

When people understand and buy into the standards, they often take on the role of self-disciplinarian.

Standards can help minimize ego issues, too. When we conduct our creative thinking workshops, we usually start out by establishing the standards and guidelines that the team will be following. This way, nobody gets offended if we decide that something doesn't work because it doesn't support a standard.

The secret is in setting up parameters ahead of time. People don't take change negatively when they know what the standards are and see how the proposed change fits into those standards. When we correct a behavior without an agreed-upon standard, people often misunderstand and resist.

Guideline #3: Intelligent, comprehensible standards become personal responsibilities.

When agreed upon, intelligently crafted standards become more than rules to follow, they become meaningful personal responsibilities for everyone who accepts them. Mere rule-followers get beaten by committed, principled people who assume responsibility every time.

A woman is said to have asked Benjamin Franklin, shortly after the drafting of the U.S. Constitution, what form the new nation would take. "A republic, madam," Franklin responded, "if you can keep it." Benjamin Franklin and the rest of the Founding Fathers understood that the most high-minded sentiments in the world are worthless if the people whom they touch lose sight of the idea of personal commitment. If the standards are such that people lose sight of their own responsibility, problems are likely to arise.

Sometimes, there are likely to be big problems. Can you imagine what it's like volunteering to make a speech in a prison, before a group of 100 murderers sentenced to life behind bars? Mike doesn't have to imagine; he did it once, a long time ago. He admits that as he began his talk before the prisoners, he was scared. What do you say to a group that includes people who have committed multiple murders? Well, Mike said, "You know, I really am scared today because I know you have all killed somebody."

The prisoners just looked at him. He went on. "And the truth of the matter is, I don't want you to kill me."

From the back of the room, there was the sound of a person laughing. Then a huge man strode toward to the podium. Mike's heart was racing. As he recalls it, this gentleman was about 6'8", with hands the size of flip charts. The fellow said, "You talk about whatever you want to talk about. Nobody's going to kill you." Talk about an important group ally!

Much relieved, Mike went on with his presentation.

After the talk, that same man took a walk with Mike around the prison exercise yard. He said, "Mike, some of the ideas you talked about really hit home with me. I never really had any standards. My parents always excused me. It didn't seem to matter how deeply I got into trouble. Nothing was ever my fault. My dad would cover up for me. He never let me fail. He never let me learn what you just said—that you have to be responsible for the consequences of your behavior. That's why I'm in this prison for the rest of my life."

Knowing the appropriate standards and taking responsibility for them are essential prerequisites to breaking through the personal limitations—the prison walls, if you will—that all people face.

These days, companies are looking for employees who display an entrepreneurial spirit, who are focused on delivering results rather than memorizing rule books. Doesn't that equate to the notion of taking responsibility for one's own behavior, fulfilling one's own obligations, making commitments?

Clearly defined standards are essential to the assumption of accountability. Will you always hit the mark? Probably not. Should you learn from each time you come up short and focus once again on your ideal, hopefully with greater wisdom? Absolutely. When you come right down to it, the Constitution—the very document Franklin tied not to formal legalisms, but to personal commitment—

represents the best kind of standard: one that is flexible but solidly grounded in principle, one that is continually appealed to and one that inspires the people it governs to summon up their best rather than their worst.

Guideline #4: Effective standards are not to be confused with a dictatorial or an authoritarian mind-set.

Appealing to standards doesn't mean being a dictator. Some people do manage to mix a healthy dose of drill sergeant into their workplace persona but never lose sight of an underlying compassion and a sense of shared responsibility. But those aren't the people we're talking about here.

Exteriors can be deceiving. One legendary "tough" executive we know of has a remarkable habit of doling out quite unexpected barrages of personal praise and support; he once grabbed Mike by the shoulders after a seminar and said, "I want you to know something—I love you." Mike later learned that this supposed "tough customer" had a way of inspiring his key managers with this brand of sudden, intense reinforcement and affection!

Standards should reflect high values and high conviction, just as that executive's did. There's nothing wrong with drawing attention to those values and convictions in a dramatic way, but if sarcasm and barking orders constitute the dominant approach to management, then you might as well not bother.

Remember that standards only work if they are accepted by others. Remember, too, that standards change over time. When you encounter a challenge that seems to defy the accepted standard, perhaps a new standard is in order. Reacting intelligently to a new situation, while keeping with your core values, is not the same as compromising.

We say: Don't sanction incompetence. This means don't cover incompetence up or walk away from it. Take responsibility for it, and help all who need to grow in a particular area take responsibility for their growth, too.

Terrorizing people isn't the best way to encourage growth. You'll only scare them to death and turn them into zombies.

We have seen plenty of examples of incompetence in the business world today, but a commitment to not sanctioning incompetence doesn't mean flying off the handle every time you encounter it in yourself or in the people with whom you work! Human beings learn through error. That means that, in most cases, you have to give people the right to experiment and, yes, even to fail.

This is true in most cases. But, of course, if a toddler is crawling toward the window in a 10-story building, the emphasis quickly shifts from letting the baby enjoy a learning experience to rescuing the baby immediately. That said, remember that such emergency instances are rare. So, resolve to give people (and yourself) a second and third chance to meet the standard. In this way, you teach people how not to fail. It's not easy, but it's the only approach that works.

So, can you take high standards and mount a crusade around them? Questions like these are best answered with actions. Just make it clear that it's not one person's idea or will, but the commitment to the standards behind the mission, that really counts!

The real-world impact of two kinds of standards

The first kind: Some time ago, Mike was at an amusement park. He asked an employee where he could find the restroom. The young woman he asked informed him that, because she had only been working there for two weeks, she was unable to tell him where he could find the restroom. She walked away. (He found himself wondering where *she* went when she had to go!)

The second kind: There was, at Disneyland, a streetsweeper named Lukie. He swept up behind the horses that go down Main Street...and you know what *he* was sweeping! Mike once saw an adult visitor with two small children walk up to Lukie and ask where he could find the restroom. Here's what Lukie said:

"Yes, sir, the restroom is right down by the flower shop. Go right in by the flower shop, immediately to the left. It's just down the street there, you see? And by the way, when you do stop in, the lady who runs the flower shop is named Anne. Please tell her Lukie said hello. She'll point you in the right direction. By the way, those are pretty little girls you have. Where are you folks from? Terre Haute, Indiana? Well, we're glad to welcome you to Disneyland. I just want to let you know that at 5 p.m. you want to be sure to catch the Disneyland parade and the lowering of the flag. Drop by and say hello again if you have the time. I hope you folks have a really nice day."

Then he tipped his hat and walked down the street.

The first story is a perfect example of a failure because of *no* standard. Conversely, the standard Lukie upheld—to treat all guests courteously and as though they were honored visitors to one's own home—is a perfect example of a standard that has been carried through to perfection.

Breakthroughs—and the superior results that accompany them—need strong standards as their foundation!

The Value Chain

The Value	The Standard	The Goal
"A value is what we believe in."	*"Standards uphold values."*	*"Goals are the desired end results."*
I. Belief in a respect for life (reverence for life) i.e., pet goldfish in pond	1. Don't eat the goldfish.	1. Living goldfish remain uneaten by small boys.
II. Right to personal property i.e., beautiful diamond ring	2. Don't steal, even if in need.	2. Person keeps his or her personal property.
III. Maintaining a creative climate	3. Provide a resource-rich environment.	3. Products and solutions are innovative.
IV. Caring for people in our company	4. Don't put people down.	4. People are motivated.

Standard Guidelines

A. Standards should tie values to goals.

B. A standard should not contradict a value.

C. There should be consequences for violating standards.

D. There should be alternatives to consider before violating standards.

E. There should be specific reasons for people to violate standards.

Summary

➤ Four important guidelines help determine and implement standards, which are the guiding imperatives that help you measure your progress toward specific goals:

1. Standards are reflections of underlying values.

2. Leadership without set standards has little or no effect.

3. Intelligent, comprehensible standards become personal responsibilities.

4. Effective standards are not to be confused with a dictatorial or an authoritarian mind-set.

➤ Standards that are carried through have far more impact than those that are simply talked about or not fully developed. The latter can be considered failed standards.

Profile: Standards

Mae Carden

Founder and Teacher, the Carden Schools

Mike feels that Mae Carden was a great teacher who influenced every life she touched. No one who sat at her knee as a pupil will ever forget her teachings or be an ordinary student. No one who sat in her classroom as a teacher in training will ever forget her or be an ordinary teacher. No one who dined with her will ever forget the rare, choice experience or be the same person after an exposure to her true elegance.

Her most extraordinary asset was that she touched people in a remarkable way— at the core of their being. She fascinated Mike and challenged him to be more than average. She said, "Don't be ordinary. Don't be average. We already have enough of ordinary and average. Always put your best side forward. Never draw attention to your weaknesses, but quietly seek to improve them."

The Carden Method

The Carden Method is a curriculum Mae Carden created for grades 1 through 12 that is used by more than 200 Carden-affiliated schools. Their success with students is legendary. They are a superlative example of how to go about establishing standards.

Thelma Sitton, early head of The View Point School in Calabassas, California, a Carden School, said of Mae Carden, "Her valiant, spirited, inspiring intellect beamed a message of hope, an impetus to teaching and learning that was matchless."

There have been hundreds of educators who have created outstanding curriculums for children. There are only a few, however, who stand the test of time. Maria Montessori and Mae Carden are two of the most distinguished. Their collective impact is without equal in the annals of teaching. Mike considers himself fortunate to have known Mae Carden and learned from her about creative teaching concepts. Undoubtedly, Mike feels that he was a better Dean of Disney University because of what she taught him during the numerous occasions they were together. As a matter of fact, Mike adopted her primary principle as part of the philosophical foundation for the training courses at the Walt Disney Company. Yes, Mae Carden even made an intellectual contribution to Disneyland!

Most important, Mae Carden embodied the values that she talked about to others, including once on a memorable trip to the Los Angeles Playboy Club on Sunset Boulevard. She even impressed the Playboy Bunnies with her sophistication and contagious charm. Her repartee didn't come from a training manual, or from sheets put together by people in human resources—it was authentic.

Learning principles: The Huntington Hotel

Mike joined Mae Carden for tea one afternoon before a lecture at the stately Huntington Hotel in Pasadena, California. What she told Mike then he's used in his career at Disney and later in his own business endeavors. He's also taught the insights to thousands of people at his seminars. Mae Carden said, "A teacher's success is, of course, measured by how much pupils learn. To find out how much they have learned, let your pupils reteach you what you taught to them. In this way, you can realistically evaluate by experience what they have learned. This is better than a formal test; it's an experience test!"

Later, when Mike designed General Electric's Maintenance and Learning Center in Erie, Pennsylvania, he taught and highly recommended the use of this Reteaching Principle. In the Reteaching Principle, students are given approximately one hour at the end of the day to prepare a briefing on Displayed Thinking boards in their Team Centers (methods we discuss in detail in Chapter 5), reviewing the essence of what they've been taught throughout the day. Their teachers, or professors, listen to the briefing, learning immediately how effective their classroom work has been. Mike and his staff also used this concept at the Disney University. It proved to be a powerful tool for increasing retention and understanding of course material. This practice is a participatory, interactive method that gets results!

The television program

Mae Carden appeared on Mike's television program in Los Angeles with four college students: Jim Whitsett, Diane Luck, Bill Boler and Ann Morgan. She had a wonderful time answering their questions. Here are some examples of her wisdom:

- ◆ One must play fair in all relationships. The price of not playing fair is the loss of inner peace.
- ◆ We cannot conceal our thoughts—they are written on our faces—so we must think better thoughts.
- ◆ What you are should always be greater than what you know.

She then enumerated the Carden Golden Rules for getting along with people:

1. Do not ask personal questions of others. They are both irritating and out of place.
2. Do not discuss your physical problems with others.
3. Keep your personal affairs to yourself.
4. Keep your conversation on subjects of general interest.
5. When someone reveals a confidence to you, keep it a confidence.
6. Do not indulge in petty gossip.
7. Let your example speak louder than your words.
8. Listen when others speak to you.

These simple maxims have profound effects when they are incorporated into anyone's set of personal values. Mike has found in his own life that when he violates one of these Carden Golden Rules it always causes problems for him.

Miss Carden was an outstanding guest on Mike's program in Los Angeles. His boss at Disney, Card Walker, happened to view her performance, and as a result he suggested having her speak at the studio to a Management Development Group. Mike and Card Walker thought she might have suggestions for a project they were working on for the proposed EPCOT Center at Disney World, studying educational concepts for the future.

She readily agreed to do this. Mike and Miss Carden had a lengthy, in-depth discussion together about educational theory and the unique teaching methods she had pioneered in her schools. Ideas they developed together proved to be really helpful to Mike when he became Dean of Disney University just a few months later.

Miss Carden talked with Mike for several hours, specifically about the importance of pupils being ready to hear what the teacher is teaching. This "teaching moment," or use of the right timing in one-on-one education, has been emphasized in the methods of many reputable educators. Pupils' minds must be open and receptive to the ideas being taught if they are to become part of their habit system.

Mike asked Miss Carden if they could explore methods or techniques that we might use to make certain the "teaching moment" was at hand during our own teaching. She was very eager to discuss this problem, and asked if Mike had any ideas in mind. He suggested that before teaching anything, a teacher could have a student experience the end results of what was going to be taught. In other words, encourage, through direct experience, an understanding of the cause behind the effect one hoped to achieve. For example, a person in training for the position of a front desk clerk in a hotel could, as the introductory step, go to the hotel and actually go through the experience of being checked in and then learn how that experience was achieved.

Mae Carden agreed with Mike's idea, but quickly pointed out that pupils also need a model of behavior from someone expert in what is being taught.

Work-Teach-Model

Mike suggested calling this the Work-Teach-Model (W-T-M) sequence. This process would reinforce learning by experiencing first, then by being taught the causes behind the experience and finally by observing a model performance of the task to be learned. This process furthers participation of the students, because, during the Work phase, they observe the details that lead to questions. Students who don't participate in classroom discourse often have no experience to base their questions on when asked to contribute.

Thus, the W-T-M sequence was created. This was an idea Mike used in designing training courses at Disney University and later for other clients. He used this concept in setting up the culture at Apple Computer, which then became part of the driving force of the culture there.

Work (experience, use, demonstrate the task)—**The effect**

Teach (explain and answer questions)—**The cause**

Model (demonstrate best practices)—**The example**

The W-T-M sequence helped develop better students, people who really understood the lesson, people who were capable of breaking out of the box.

Mike had the privilege of attending a Carden teachers' training lecture at The Viewpoint School in California. Miss Carden sat on a riser in the front of the room, speaking and fielding a barrage of questions from many highly motivated teachers.

One teacher asked her why her textbooks had no pictures or drawings in them since most other texts have so many pictures. Miss Carden replied, "Children learn to read the written word without graphic clues this way. Pictures become crutches that hurt reading skills. Children never forget what they understand. They forget what they memorize."

A young teacher asked Miss Carden to outline the purpose of the Carden Method. What was the mission that she believed in for her schools? Here's the answer Miss Carden gave:

The new purpose in teaching

The purpose of the Carden Method is to develop

adjusted,

capable,

confident,

eager,

alert,

courageous,

generous,

just,

self-critical,

compassionate,

courteous,

happy

children...

...children who have a sense of humor, who will be able to develop their ingenuity, who base their actions on the idea that we came to life to make a contribution to the welfare of the human race; children who realize that happiness is a by-product of doing for others, children who realize that the goal of living is not the amassing of money or possessions but the attainment of the desires of the heart.

"If we would develop these values," Miss Carden continued, "the result would be more persons who break out of themselves." She said, "I'm not interested in Mae Carden. I'm interested in saving children. We should strive for strength of character and a deep sense of personal responsibility in our pupils."

There were many questions about leadership, both in education and business, that she addressed with alacrity, even after a long day of teaching. "When a mother says that it is easier to do it herself," Miss Carden observed, "she is failing as a parent. When managers say that it is easier to do it themselves, they too are failing as managers. I don't mind when pupils make errors because it's an opportunity to teach them. Avoid going off in every direction. Let a pupil learn one thing well before proceeding to the next thing."

You can understand why this woman was such an effective teacher. Her methods were based on values that were constructive, as well as teachable. She once observed, "I am never after merely the right answer, but the mental process that produces the answer."

Mae Carden's Breakout Qualities

- Setting examples
- Presenting her best side
- Maintaining dignity
- Letting pupils reteach
- Showing curiosity about the unknown
- Showing acceptance of others as they are

BREAKTHROUGH TECHNIQUES

TRANSLATING VALUES INTO GOALS

☑ List at least three vital standards that are absolutely essential to achieve a breakthrough on your project or problem.

☑ Relate these three standards to the three values they represent. (See Chapter 10 for an in-depth discussion of values.) Values and standards that are in synch and compatible offer a greater chance for breakthroughs. Prepare a comparison column between values and standards. Who is responsible for doing this?

☑ Establish specific goals for your project. What are they? Are the goals a true reflection of your listed values, laid out as described above?

☑ Project what possible breakthroughs would help you achieve your goals. Write a description of the breakthroughs you're looking for. Do you have a description of the problem or needs surrounding a possible breakthrough?

☑ Plot out your values, standards and goals in relationship to each other. Keep track of the progress; indicate what has been achieved and completed

☑ Research the past to understand where the breakthroughs have been in your company or industry. What were the circumstances that provided a need? Who made the breakthroughs? How did it happen? How was it implemented? Are the guiding principles still valid?

☑ What are the driving factors in your industry? What do you anticipate they will be in the future?

CHAPTER 3

Managing Yourself and Others

"I've never met an ugly person, only a lazy one."

—Helena Rubinstein

Management—of yourself and others—remains a fine art, one that takes time to master. Even in this era of highly developed technology, finding constructive ways to work with people is a real challenge. During a visit we had with the late J.W. Marriott at the Camelback Inn in Phoenix, Arizona, he told us what he felt was an effective definition of the word "management" in today's business environment: "I think management is the ability to get work done through people—while having fun!"

The way people think, feel and talk about management has undergone profound changes in recent years, as Mr. Marriott's definition reveals. People have gone in every direction, followed any number of theories, explored every new idea. Fortunately, out of this maze of thinking, some exciting, enlightened new ideas have emerged.

There are many books on management, offering differing perspectives to consider in developing an effective philosophy of personal leadership. No one would (or could) try to follow all the advice within the covers of these books. That would turn readers into schizophrenics. But there are certainly some valuable insights to be gained. There are a few classics worthy of just about anyone's time and attention. One is Peter Drucker's *The Effective Executive*. It offers explicit, usable examples of how to be an effective executive and leader.

But this book is the rare exception. The vast majority of these books simply don't go deep enough. Too many of them may help diagnose a problem but fail to help find a solution. And they can't be too helpful when they cause constant shifting from last month's hot philosophy toward this month's latest offering! Most people find that constantly trying to adopt the latest management principle can be both personally stressful as well as confusing to everyone in the organization. What's desirable isn't one big, new, overriding idea for management, but a series of effective concepts that are adaptable to a variety of managerial approaches.

Managing while having fun

An enlightened approach to leadership requires us to define management as the ability to help people enjoy developing their own talents and reach a state of personal fulfillment. *Management can be fun!*

There are other definitions of management that have become popular over the years. If you're operating under one of these systems, the six techniques in this chapter can be adapted to your approach. People may need to change their terminologies and thinking, but in most cases that's not the most critical issue. The important goal is to have everyone participate.

Other definitions of management

The *cooperative focus on constructive goals,* with an emphasis on *fun,* is the emerging way of defining management, but it's certainly not the only way.

One of the most popular management styles has been a "my way or the highway" approach, in which the manager points the troops toward a certain goal, then pushes, pulls, shoves and kicks until his wishes are carried out. If none of that works, the superior usually offers nothing new for a substitute approach and simply gets rid of the offenders. This is called dictatorship, authoritarianism or M.B.B.A.S.O.B., which stands for "management by being a..." — well, you get the idea.

Mike was trained in the infantry. The guiding philosophy of the rifle company in Korea where he was stationed was "my way or the highway" because of the operating conditions; if you failed to deliver on what your superior wanted, you often risked getting killed! In the corporate environment, this management style has fallen out of favor in recent years, but there's a secret about it that people rarely discuss: It *does* get things done — in the short term.

"My way or the highway" can deliver impressive results. It can also cause people to be demotivated, a fact that has its own implications.

"My way or the highway" management can burn people out if it is over-used. It discourages personal initiative. No matter what results it may deliver in the short term, it doesn't succeed as the only management philosophy, but not everyone has realized this yet. People should be treated respectfully, not like slaves. Their thinking must become part of the solution. Top people should interact with others to get at the *causes* of problems and situations.

Management defined as *the ability to get work done through people* hasn't been subject to as much criticism as the "my way or the highway" approach. Viewing management as the ability to *facilitate cooperation* among people seeking to achieve constructive goals helps appeal to people's deeper values and points them in a positive direction. This way of operating can be adapted to a situation in which the manager is a *participant,* not merely an issuer of orders.

Helping people by instilling a cooperative effort toward the achievement of constructive goals—and leading by personal example—is the most successful management approach.

The focus should not be on a rigid hierarchy—or on vague ideas of "development"—but on results. The manager becomes the facilitator, the person who stimulates growth and motivation among others.

What are the major characteristics of an effective facilitator of breakthroughs? There are six, each of which can be adapted to virtually any challenge you face. What's more, each enhances the ability to interact creatively with others.

The breakthrough facilitator practices respect for the individual.

We will look at mutual respect in detail later, but it's important to discuss it briefly now because it has a dramatic effect on the way people observe themselves and others, as well as on the quality of breakthroughs they achieve.

The breakthrough facilitator understands that people have to manage themselves, especially in this high-tech age. The higher the technology people are expected to master, the more their own self-management becomes an essential precondition of the workplace.

That's true for us, and it's true for the people who work with us. The ability to master staggering amounts of information through modern technology allows people to be "in the know" about a vast amount of data. As a result, they should receive respect and autonomy. Environments of respect foster high achievement and success.

A facilitator of breakthroughs demonstrates to everyone how to think as management would think, as an entrepreneur would think. The most propitious way to achieve the spirit of this mind-set is to ensure an environment of respect by truly listening to what others have to say, not just attending to conversations in a perfunctory way.

The person who practices mutual respect exemplifies the characteristics of effective self-managers, people who act as internal entrepreneurs. Mutual respect is also one of the characteristics of an empathetic team player. Among the positive effects is that it prepares people for early supervisory and management assignments.

Managers will often complain they don't have enough resources to supervise everybody. It can be a valid complaint. However, if managers respect people and appreciate their intelligence and individuality enough, they encourage them to supervise themselves. Companies can enjoy superb results from this initiative to build a favorable climate for growth. Organizations in which people are responsible for practicing self-management have high achievement records.

The breakthrough facilitator acts as a catalyst for change and achievement.

Breakthrough facilitators are on the move, leading others toward accomplishment. This is known as "walk-around management," a term first associated with Walt Disney's leadership style. It's been a part of the practical, dramatic style of inspiring leaders for years. Thomas Edison walked around a lot, forever poking into activities and posing the questions that helped his people. Just as important, this technique also helped Edison himself look at problems in a new light.

Walt Disney played the role of the catalyst at his studio. A child once asked Disney exactly what it was he did around the place. Disney thought for a moment, then said, "I'll tell you what I do. I'm a bumblebee. I fly around spreading pollen from place to place all over the studio. Sometimes I have to go back and spread some more pollen around. Sometimes I have to get other people to do it. But that's basically what I do. I spread pollen."

Bumblebees facilitate breakthroughs that benefit everyone!

Peter Drucker called this bumblebee analogy one of the finest he'd ever heard. Notice Disney didn't say that he spent all day telling people what to do.

Organizations sometimes have what should be called "walk-*by* management" (as opposed to "walk-*around* management"), the kind of superficial "leadership" in which an executive walks by and drops a bomb on the project. Then he or she walks out, having trashed the team's efforts. That's the *opposite* of bumblebee facilitating. Bumblebee facilitating encourages people rather than discourages them. It allows them to participate.

The idea of the Borrowed Hero helps to maintain a participative climate. This practice involves selecting an inspiring authority as a model for people to consider and measuring their creative efforts against this Borrowed Hero's likely approach to a problem—instead of the founder's or president's. For example, Walt Disney would often ask, "How would Leonardo da Vinci do this?" Which approach do *you* think is likely to lead to a more creative outcome: asking, "How would Leonardo have done this?" or saying, "I really don't think that's going to work"?

Breakthrough facilitators face issues realistically.

Breakthrough facilitators don't walk away from difficult issues. They don't avoid confrontation by attempting to bury problems. That's a hallmark of the authoritarian approach, which often results in distorted information.

In our seminars, we often talk about managers who don't face issues. We call them practitioners of "snake-in-the-grass management." If you watch a snake move around on the ground, you'll see that it moves from side to side to go forward. Scientists call this "precession." Unfortunately, it isn't limited to snakes. Too many *people*, managers and nonmanagers alike, practice the habit of precession. They see a controversial issue coming, and they avoid it, hoping they won't have to take a side. They see another one coming, and they avoid taking sides again. They believe that if they avoid dealing with pressing questions, they can keep from having to disagree with anyone.

People only fool themselves with snake-in-the-grass maneuvers! Important problems don't get solved. Breakthroughs come in environments where people are realistic, where they avoid phoniness and posturing.

Breakthrough facilitators promote participation, but don't do the "sidestep" when making final decisions.

Facilitators who achieve breakthroughs instinctively love and encourage participation. They understand that, as Walt Disney often said, "There's no corner on brains." He knew that *everyone* has the potential for achieving breakthrough thinking, and he took full advantage of the potential of his people.

Ideally, decisions should be made with the full benefit of participation from various members of the organization, but promoting participation is *not* necessarily synonymous with embracing a completely participatory decision-making style. Leaders have differing opinions on the merits of participatory decision-making. We believe participative management can be helpful when used at the appropriate time. We also believe that, at the end of the day, *someone* must be accountable for having made a decision, because when "no one" is responsible, *everyone* may become responsible.

Approached correctly, participation can yield high productivity. Creative input is likely to lead to creative outcomes. But in effective organizations, the final decision to *implement* ideas is usually sanctioned by an individual; participative management doesn't work by simply doing whatever group consensus suggests. There's probably nothing you can do that other people *can't* participate in, but accountability for what you do can't be placed in the hands of 50 different people. It has to remain with you.

Managers sometimes find that no one on the team is willing to assume responsibility for a failed initiative. Failure leaves a bad taste—and the result is overreaction. Companies move in the opposite direction, and allow *no* participation, thereby wasting talent! Much of that waste can be prevented when the right person assumes personal responsibility for the decision and gives people the right to fail. In truly participative management, members don't fear reprisals for failure; they just step up to the plate again.

Sometimes, the best decision may be to ask your people to go back and get more information. Intelligently employed, this technique does not represent a bureaucratic dodge, but a strategic way of bringing about a breakthrough! Asking for more data gives you the opportunity to promote participation to make a better decision, without sidestepping the act of decision-making itself.

Breakthrough facilitators understand that there are times when you have to be authoritarian.

Being *selectively* authoritarian is not the same as being brutal and dictatorial in every situation. Sometimes an authoritarian response is the only appropriate one. On the other hand, sometimes authoritarianism is completely inappropriate.

How do you know when to exercise authoritarianism?

The answer to this question has to do with standards. There are situations in which a specific standard is at issue, a standard everyone knows well and has vowed to uphold, and people can work on reaching that standard *as they see fit. A standard that is specific enough can be upheld by individuals on their own initiative.* But there are also situations in which that standard is in danger of being violated, with potentially catastrophic results. In such a case, you need to take action fast. You need to act decisively. You have to take a *temporary* authoritarian stance to avoid a crisis. In such a situation, authoritarianism is not an option but an imperative. When the danger has passed, you revert to a participative frame of mind. For example, when a pilot discovers that an engine in his plane is on fire, he will be authoritarian in his demeanor and take whatever steps are necessary to get his team to focus on the task at hand and support him as he tries to land the plane safely.

The head of a state police system told Mike that an authoritarian mind-set should kick in only in dangerous situations where physical harm is imminent, but *isn't* necessary in other situations. This is an example of *temporary* authoritarianism—used only until a crisis has subsided. In other words, once the danger has passed, you move *away* from the authoritarian mind-set (also known as the Theory X mind-set), in which you tell people what they must do, usually in order to maintain a certain standard. You move back to the participative mind-set (also known as the Theory Y mind-set), in which you devote your time to analyzing factors that caused the problem, often as part of a team effort.

If you skip the Y method, you often miss out on breakthroughs! But if you make the participative approach your normal operating procedure, deviating from it only when crisis looms, you will earn a reputation as a person who takes action to uphold a standard.

Do you remember our example about the baby in the window? If a toddler is about to fall out of the open window of a 10-story building, you don't put together a team and employ collaborative management so you can decide what to do about the situation. You restrain the toddler—that is, take an approach that is 100 percent authoritarian—because this is the appropriate response in this dangerous situation. On the other hand, if it was a teenager struggling over personal values (but not in imminent physical danger), attempting to "tell the kid what to do" usually will not work. In this case, you need to help the teenager in a participative way that encourages sound personal decision-making.

Selective authoritarianism does not excuse or justify uncontrolled aggressiveness. Actions in defense of the maintenance of standards during times of crisis do not require being a harsh person. (Bear in mind that responding harshly, even to harsh and hostile people, usually doesn't get you very far.)

People can act decisively without being jerks!

When you work within the X framework, you take temporary action to deal with a potentially catastrophic *effect*, not a cause. When you swing back to the Y framework, you then deal with underlying forces that *caused* the problem.

At Disneyland, big workhorses are used to pull the trolley cars up and down Main Street. Some years back, a Disneyland employee tried to use a shortcut to take the horses back to the pony farm for a rest. This ill-considered path led the exhausted horses directly to a huge, oncoming, teeming crowd of visitors—many of whom were holding small children by the hand.

The shortcut was more than a bad idea. It was a dangerous idea. Suppose the horses had panicked? Suppose children had gotten hurt? The decision to take a shortcut led to a clear situation where authoritarian action was required.

Fortunately, an appropriate response came from a senior official who worked in the operations department (with whom Mike happened to be walking at the time). He immediately assumed control of the situation by grabbing the horses, turning them around and shouting, "Let's go the other way!" The horses did.

The operations man acted in an authoritarian way to head off the danger. But once the danger had passed, he said clearly, but not at all threateningly, to the employee who took the shortcut, "I would like you to take the horses back to the pony farm by their normal route, and then I'd like to meet with you in my office, and I'd like to talk with you about why this happened."

In a split second he had gone from X to Y because he wanted to uncover the *cause* of the problem. He wanted to make sure that what had happened would never happen again. He knew he had to facilitate interaction among the team members who had supported the suggestion to take the ill-advised shortcut. So he arranged to talk with them (not to browbeat them) and get their input on a plan to make certain this problem didn't recur.

Breakthrough thinking adapts easily from the rare instances that require authoritarian X thinking to the more common instances when participative Y thinking is appropriate. The mature leader understands the concepts behind each style and is flexible, moving easily between the two.

Breakthrough facilitators are truthful.

To be a breakthrough facilitator, you have to be truthful.

Do you remember the first *Superman* movie? It contains one of finest management concepts we've ever heard. You may recall the poignant scene in which Lois Lane and Superman are out flying, having a grand time, and then they land on her balcony. Lois says to Superman, "I want to ask you a question—what do you believe in?" The question somewhat shocks him.

"I believe," he answers, "in truth, justice and the American way."

That's a great line, and it makes a great management philosophy, whether people think they know all about truth, justice and the American way or are a little bit skeptical about such notions.

Lois Lane is certainly skeptical. She says, "You're putting me on, right?" Then Superman adds the other major point essential to any facilitator of breakthroughs. He says, "Lois, I never lie." (One child in the audience at the theater where Mike first saw the film said, "I wish my parents were like that.")

We once asked the managers of a large company why they didn't practice Superman management. In other words, why not make a pledge to tell the truth to all distributors, customers, suppliers and employees? Why not pledge always to be just and fair with them? Why not make a commitment to reward initiative and inventiveness? After all, it's the American way to make honesty, fair dealing and hard work the foundations of group and individual success!

They just stared at us in disbelief. We thought they were going to jump right out of their wingtip shoes. The president of the company said, "It would destroy the company!"

We couldn't believe it. We wondered: *Would* Superman's standard have destroyed the company, or would it have told people that they worked at the kind of company where they could count on a square deal—the kind of company where real, meaningful breakthroughs were openly celebrated and fairly rewarded?

The world needs more breakthrough facilitators

No matter what the stated philosophy at the organization for which you work, the six ideas we've just outlined can help you get the most from yourself and others. They'll help you summon breakthroughs that tame little problems before they grow. That beats burying the problems and covering them up, because buried problems have a way of resurfacing!

Use the ideas in this chapter whether you're facilitating a project group, heading up an idea-generating session or simply trying to work more effectively

THE LIFE CYCLE OF LEARNING

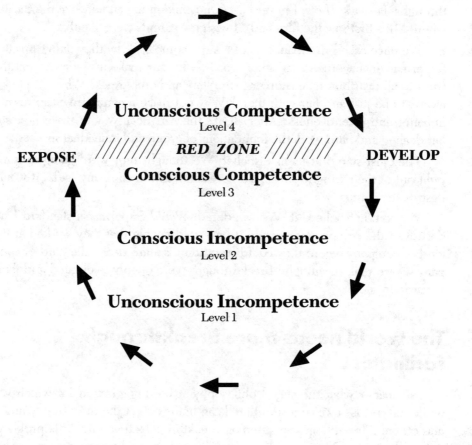

Unconscious Competence
Level 4

EXPOSE ///////// *RED ZONE* ///////// DEVELOP

Conscious Competence
Level 3

Conscious Incompetence
Level 2

Unconscious Incompetence
Level 1

with the other members of your team. Practice them! Improve your technique! Enter Maslow's "red zone"!

The red zone

The psychologist Abraham Maslow outlined four now-famous levels of learning. Here they are:

1. Unconscious incompetence, in which people don't yet know that they don't know what they're doing.

2. Conscious incompetence, in which they're aware that they don't yet know what they're doing.

3. Conscious competence, in which they know how to do what needs to be done.

4. Unconscious competence, in which they do what needs to be done so well they do it automatically.

Dr. Maslow lectured at Disney University. During one of his talks he added something to the four-tiered system, something that Walt Disney especially liked and that Mike added to the Disney management development program. Maslow drew red slash marks between the top two levels (conscious competence and unconscious competence), thereby identifying a "red zone" in which people *move* from knowing they know to effortless, instinctive ability. (See the figure on page 64.) That's the essential transitional phase, the zone you want to enter and pass through, but not spend too much time in. If you spend too much time in the "red zone," it means you're not moving through the cycle of continuous learning.

In managing yourself—the most important prerequisite to managing others—one of the most critical commitments you can make is to develop your existing skills continually. That's a big part of breaking out of the box. The idea is to expose yourself to new challenges in an ongoing effort to move through the red zone into new areas that require further learning.

Note that we said *an ongoing effort*. When does the effort to find some new red zone stop? Never! Not if you want to launch a revival. Not it you want to break out of the box.

65

Summary

➤ Management defined as the ability to get people to realize their maximum potential through work while having fun is one of the most constructive approaches you can take to leadership.

➤ "My way or the highway" management is another approach. It can deliver results, but it has a way of demotivating people if it is overused. This style of management is not very good at getting at the causes of problems.

➤ We think of a manager as a facilitator of breakthroughs. There are six major characteristics of a good facilitator of breakthroughs:

1. The breakthrough facilitator practices respect for the individual.

2. The breakthrough facilitator acts as a catalyst for change and achievement.

3. The breakthrough facilitator faces issues realistically.

4. The breakthrough facilitator promotes participation, but doesn't "sidestep" when making final decisions.

5. The breakthrough facilitator understands that there are times when only an authoritarian approach is appropriate.

6. The breakthrough facilitator is truthful.

➤ There is no substitute for a "Superman" management philosophy that embraces truth, justice and the American way!

➤ Breakthrough facilitators must continually expose themselves to new "red zones." That is, they must continually expose themselves to new challenges and the development of new skills.

Profile: Managing Yourself and Others

J. Willard Marriott

The Marriott Corporation, Founder

We both knew the dynamic, energetic J. Willard Marriott—a remarkable man who was called Bill by his close friends, "Montana Marriott" by his oldest friends and Mr. Marriott by just about everyone else.

His success story was that of a farm boy who made good in the big city. He was the consummate entrepreneur, a 20th-century Horatio Alger character. He was also the kind of man you just couldn't help liking.

Like virtually everyone else who met him, we, too, liked Mr. Marriott a great deal; we always heard wise words and counsel from him.

Mike first met the industrious Mr. Marriott during a speaking engagement at the Twin Bridges Marriott Hotel in Washington, D.C. Mike Hostage, the president of Marriott at the time, was holding a manager's meeting.

Mike Vance noticed, during his own talk with the managers, a man who was sitting in the front row on the far right, taking notes faster than Mike was talking. His pencil seemed to be flying across the yellow tablets that were set up in front of him. In his entire speaking career, Mike had never seen anyone take notes the way this man did; he was recording important points on *two* yellow tablets, and with both hands! Mike was very intrigued by the man.

The first mid-morning break presented Mike with an opportunity to meet this mysterious man. He asked Mike Hostage to introduce him to the fast-writing gentleman. They walked over to him, and Hostage said, "Mike, I'd like you to meet J. Willard Marriott."

That was one of the few times in his life that Mike Vance was nearly speechless. He had not recognized the famed business leader who was sitting in his audience.

After the introductions and greetings, J. Willard Marriott said to Mike, "I am enjoying your talk very much."

Mike said, "I noticed that you're taking notes on two yellow tablets. Do you always do that?"

"Naw," Mr. Marriott said genially. "On one tablet I was writing what you were saying, and on the other I was writing what I'm going to do about it. If you'll excuse me, Mike, I'm going to get my wife so she can hear the rest of your talk. I'll be back..."

That was the extent of Mike's first encounter with J.Willard Marriott. It would not be the last. Mike came to develop a profound respect for the man.

The Peace Pipe Room at the Camelback Inn

Mike had told Diane a number of stories about J. Willard Marriott, stories that illustrated that he was both tough and gentle, devout and fun-loving, demanding and tolerant, frugal and philanthropic. He was also unapologetically patriotic; he fervently believed in the American dream. His own success story was an inspiring illustration of that dream. Mr. Marriott had turned a nine-stool root beer stand known as the Hot Shoppe into a series of hotels and, eventually, a huge corporate empire.

Diane's first opportunity to meet Montana Marriott came unexpectedly. Mike was the visiting speaker for a group at Marriott's Camelback Inn in Scottsdale, Arizona for a day. Diane was seated at a table in the last row near the doors. The meeting had started when a gentleman came in and sat down right beside Diane. Once again, the mysterious man began taking notes furiously. Diane knew it could only be J.W. Marriott, because Mike had told her about his unique, intense way of taking notes.

She introduced herself to him: "Mr. Marriott, I'm Diane Deacon. I'm a partner of Mike Vance. I've heard so many good things about you from Mike."

He said, "I'm happy to meet you. I never miss an opportunity to hear Mike when I can. He puts out a hundred ideas a minute."

Diane and Mr. Marriott talked periodically throughout Mike's lecture; she soon learned that Marriott, too, was full of a hundred ideas a minute.

At the first break Mr. Marriott excused himself, saying that he had to make a phone call to tell one of his family members about Mike's A Kitchen for the Mind idea. He loved the concept and wanted someone to implement it right away. When he returned, Diane said to him, "You believe in getting things done right now, don't you?"

"Yes," he said, "I try not to put anything off. Too many people defer everything to some other time. I can never understand why people do this. You can't get very much done if you always put it off until tomorrow or the next day."

It was abundantly clear to Diane how Mr. Marriott got from a root beer stand in Washington to a billion-dollar company. She stood talking with Mr. Marriott at the back of the Peace Pipe Room until Mike finished greeting the people attending his seminar. The last thing she heard him say before he left was, "Make today as perfect as you can, and tomorrow will take care of itself."

On another occasion when Mike was staying at the Camelback Marriott he got up early to enjoy the sunrise. Mike knew that a sunrise in the Arizona desert is beautiful, something one does not want to miss; and he knew that a walk through the beautiful flower gardens at the Camelback Inn is also exquisite. So he got up early enough to enable him to enjoy these pleasures before his breakfast meeting with Mr. Marriott.

Mike was walking through the grounds; it was still dark outside. No one else was up except staff members working the graveyard shift...and Mr. Marriott. There he was, among some flowerbeds, taking in their early-morning fragrance. Mr. Marriott greeted Mike, then started talking about the flowers. He explained how they had to be hearty to survive the intense heat of the hot desert sun. "It's like trees," he said. "Tough trees stand up to the strongest winds, and that means they make top-notch timber."

Mr. Marriott seemed to have a keen interest in nature, and Mike asked him what his hobbies were.

"I like ranching, hunting and fishing," he answered, "and eating Mulligan stew around a glowing campfire. I'm in love with the out-of-doors."

This remark reminded Mike of a very unusual speaking experience. Over breakfast, he shared it with Mr. Marriott.

"Some years ago," Mike told him, "I received an invitation to speak before the National Hobo Convention. The conditions were interesting, to say the least. The speech took place outside in a large open field. I arrived at dawn, walked to the middle of the field to the place I was to speak and saw more than 50 campfires burning, all tended by the members of my audience: the hoboes. They were having a contest that would be judged later that morning: Who could make the best Mulligan stew. They wanted to know who the master Mulligan stew-maker was."

Bill Marriott roared with laughter. He obviously was enjoying the story, so Mike continued.

"I was introduced to members of the group, who were sitting in semidarkness except for the flickering glow of the campfires. I found myself wondering: What exactly do you say to an audience of hoboes? I decided to say the same thing I'd say to anybody else. I thought of them as though they were a gathering of CEOs. And I gave them my grandmother's recipe for rhubarb pie, which had been a favorite among the hoboes who had visited her home in Greenville, Ohio.

"Anyway, they asked me to taste all the Mulligan stews after my talk. I wondered what some of the ingredients might be in a hobo's stew. I wasn't too keen on the answers I came up with, but I tasted the stews anyway."

Bill Marriott was laughing heartily again. He slapped his knee and said, "Mike, life is like a hobo's Mulligan stew. You never know what's going to be in there. But you have to sample it and make every bit of it count in your life. You can't waste a second."

After Mike's hobo story, the two began to talk about management and leadership.

Mike asked Mr. Marriott how he felt about the classic definition of management: management as the ability to get work done through people. Mr. Marriott answered, "It's fine. But you must add one word to make the definition work: *fun*. It should be: Management is the ability to get work done through people while having *fun*. I'm always looking for better managers. I'm looking for those who love it so much they're having fun at it. I'm looking for managers who can get along with people. Most of them really know how to have fun."

Humility

Humility was one of Bill Marriott's finest qualities. His achievements, his wealth and his influence were immense but he remained an extremely humble man throughout his life. His business philosophy was simple:

1. Render friendly service to our guests.
2. Offer quality food at a fair price.
3. Work hard day and night to make a profit.
4. Grow to create jobs for more employees.
5. Don't ever put all your eggs in one basket.

These are simple, humble ideas—but very powerful ones!

A letter to his son Bill

The greatest gift Mike received during his friendship with J.W. Marriott was the privilege of reading a letter Mr. Marriott had written to his son Bill before the younger Marriott became president of the Marriott Corporation. This letter is also contained in the book *The J. Willard Marriott Story* by Robert O'Brien (which can be found next to the Bible in most Marriott hotels):

January 20, 1964

Dear Bill:

I am mighty proud of you. Years of preparation, work and study have shown results.

A leader should have character, be an example in all things. This is his greatest influence. In this you are admirable. You have not taken advantage of your position as my son. You remain humble.

You have proved you can manage people and get them to work for you. You have made a profit—your thinking works. You are developing more patience and understanding with people, more maturity.

It is not often that a father has a son who can step into his shoes and wear them on the basis of his own accomplishments and ability. Being the operating manager of a business on which some 30,000 people depend for a livelihood is a frightening responsibility, but I have the greatest confidence you will build a team that will ensure the continued success of a business that has been borne through years of love and devotion by many wonderful people. I have written down a few guideposts—all borne out of my experience and ones I wish I could have followed more closely.

Love and best wishes.

Sincerely,
Dad

Bill's guideposts

(Written on 15 separate sheets of stationery)

1. Keep physically fit and mentally and spiritually strong.

2. Guard your habits; bad ones will destroy you.

3. Pray about every difficult problem.

4. Study and follow professional management principles. Apply them logically and practically to your organization.

5. People are number one: Develop their loyalty, interest, team spirit. Develop managers in every area. This is your prime responsibility.

6. Decisions: Men grow by making decisions and assuming responsibility for them.

    A) Make crystal clear what decisions each manager is responsible for and what decisions you reserve for yourself.

    B) Have all the facts and counsel necessary—then decide and stick to your decision.

7. Criticism: Don't criticize people; make a fair appraisal of their qualifications with their supervisor only (or someone assigned to do this). Remember, anything you say about someone may (and usually does) get back to them. There are few secrets.

8. See the good in people and try to develop those qualities.

9. Inefficiency: If it cannot be overcome, and an employee is obviously incapable of the job, find a job he can do or terminate him now. Don't wait.

10. Manage your time.

    A) Keep conversations short and to-the-point.

    B) Make every minute on the job count.

    C) Work fewer hours (some of us waste half of our time).

11. Delegate and hold others accountable for details.

12. Details:

    A) Let your staff take care of them.

    B) Save your energy for planning, thinking, working with department heads and promoting new ideas.

    C) Don't do anything someone else can do for you.

13. Ideas and competition:

    A) Remember, ideas keep the business alive.

    B) Know what your competitors are doing and planning.

    C) Encourage all managers to think about better ways to work; give suggestions on anything that will improve business.

    D) Spend time and money on research and development.

14. Don't try to do an employee's job for him or her; offer counsel and support.

15. Think objectively and keep a sense of humor, make the business fun for you and others.

This, then, is our recollection of J.W. Marriott, a truly exemplary person who serves as a model of behavior.

J.Willard Marriott's Breakout Qualities

- ◆ Absolute integrity
- ◆ Honest humility
- ◆ Ability to develop people
- ◆ Outgoing and friendly attitude
- ◆ Caring nature
- ◆ Philanthropic outlook
- ◆ Spirituality

BREAKTHROUGH TECHNIQUES

ACHIEVING MAXIMUM USE OF RESOURCES

☑ What will be the team's working method for developing the projects? Select and agree upon the method you will use. Establish rules of order to limit interruptions during Creative Thinking Sessions. What are the rules?

☑ Find out how much time is required to achieve the breakthrough. Allot time for the workshop session(s). Develop a schedule. Get commitment up front from the team to the time frame; this will help limit turnover of members.

☑ Establish what work will be done together with the team and what work will be done individually by team members. Identify who will do what work.

☑ Manage the discipline of the homework by individual team members. When and where will they do the work?

☑ Establish when members will brief the team on their individual research and conclusions.

CHAPTER 4

Maintaining a Creative Climate and Culture

"The world may be a mess, but my life doesn't need to be."
—Karl Lagerfeld

Buckminster Fuller, inventor of the geodesic dome, said many times, "The universe itself is creative, and we can be partners in this ongoing creativity."

The challenge is to maintain a creative climate and culture in people's work and living environments. The quality of environments used to promulgate breakthrough thinking has an immense impact on the originality of people's ideas. In this chapter, we'll examine proven ways to enrich your surroundings, both physical and intellectual, techniques that will lay the foundation for revival-oriented, break-out-of-the-box thinking.

Why creative thinking suffers

Often, creative thinking suffers when insufficient attention is devoted to the issue of fostering a work climate in which creativity is the norm, not the exception. Simply summoning people into the office and demanding instant results is unlikely to yield creative solutions!

You must take the time and make the effort to design a working atmosphere that supports creativity all the time. The most common obstacle to doing so is a corporate culture unwilling to change its outlook. In lieu of creative thinking, many companies have resorted to downsizing campaigns to improve the bottom line or to mergers and acquisitions instead of creating new products and services. A common justification for this type of thinking is: "Reducing the staff is the only way we can improve our productivity" or "It's quicker to acquire than it is to create." These excuses often reflect a lack of creativity and sometimes are perfect examples of "sidestepping."

There are no magic formulas or quick fixes for establishing or maintaining a creative climate and culture. However, there are some clear indications of when it's time to make changes.

7 warning signs that an existing culture needs to be changed

Let's consider the essential ways of identifying a restrictive corporate culture, then look at ways you can enhance your surroundings once you know it's time to institute change. There are seven warning signs that should make you stop and reconsider your organization's culture:

Warning sign #1: People are having difficulty accepting new ideas and adopting new technologies; they are resisting change. This is usually a clear indication that people either don't understand the new ideas because of lack of information or they fear the results of new technologies. Resistance to change is almost always motivated by fear of the unknown.

Solution: Use participation to involve people in the creation of new ideas. Conduct periodic briefings to keep everyone up-to-date on the expected changes. Face the issues head-on with open dialogue. Avoid keeping anyone in the dark.

Warning sign #2: People are bogged down in routine and fixed procedures. Routine has its place in any organization; it's often part of being well-organized. The problems begin when routine prevents people from responding effectively when circumstances change. People may fail to change direction even in the face of an oncoming avalanche because of their adherence to fixed procedures and ingrained rituals. Routine has its place—but you must know when to let go of it when circumstances demand.

Solution: Review policy procedures and routines on a regular basis, weeding out the obsolete practices and replacing them with innovations based on the new circumstances.

Warning sign #3: Poor ideas are being generated. People tend to generate poor ideas when their perspective is unrealistic. Without an appraisal of situations as they really are, the "solutions" that result are the products of insufficient research and development or no research at all.

Also, when people become sloppy or careless in their work and generate poor ideas, they may have become oversold on hype rather than the real substance behind a concept. Many ideas that sound good on the surface but deliver no results mean that a change is in order.

Solution: "Court" ideas for longer periods—don't try to turn them into "one-night stands." Do the homework. Improve the techniques being used to conduct research and development. Validate the homework with tough performance standards. Make sure the information you have is accurate and comprehensive, that it truly applies to the situations you're evaluating.

When a team is generating too many unrealistic ideas, it is time to think about changing this part of your culture. Dreams are fine, as long as they're doable. Suggest more valid, pragmatic programs.

Warning sign #4: Excessive politicking is taking place. A plethora of politicking in an organization is usually the result of too many people not playing in the game, but rather sitting on the bench with time on their hands. This situation can have a devastating impact on creativity and productivity.

When many individuals are focused on positioning, maneuvering and gossiping, there's a problem. Relationships and alliances are important—this is, after all, an era of collaboration and partnering—but the alliances should be focused on challenges faced by the team, not merely on the notion of beating out rivals within the organization.

Often, people who seem to focus on politics all the time are covering up problems, trying to use political issues as a smokescreen to conceal their lack of productivity. A bluff here, a sidestep there...a culture of full-time politicking can make any organization an undesirable place to be!

Solution: The most effective way to decrease petty politicking is to get everyone in the game. Ferret out people who are not doing very much; get them involved. Stop the goldbricking by eliminating projects that represent "busywork." Remember, too, that politicking occurs when there are not enough effective standards in place to carry out constructive values.

Warning sign #5: Few ideas are being implemented. There is nothing that will destroy a creative climate faster than a failure to implement good ideas. If the so-called "empowering" of a team results in a great plan that never gets put into action, it isn't empowering at all. It's demoralizing to everyone on the team. Teams working on projects that never turn into reality conclude that they are performing a perfunctory role and not really part of a participative culture. They are right.

Solution: Team members should be selected with care, and their positions should be clearly spelled out at the beginning of a project. Ideas can be carried out when someone has the authority to bring the team's recommendations to closure with a list of implementable steps.

Warning sign #6: Philosophies and products are becoming outdated. The philosophy of an organization determines the success or failure of its products and services. When organizations fail to update their philosophies and strategies, products and services often become moribund and outdated. Company after company has failed because of a refusal to keep up with changing times and conditions. Business analysts often point to the fact that few of the original Fortune 500 companies exist today. Most of them fell victim to this mode of thinking.

Solution: Don't stand pat. Instead, be growth-oriented. Embrace realistic expansion plans and dynamic change. Find new niches for existing product lines, and seek to keep the product line fresh.

Gary Wendt, the CEO of General Electric Capital Corporation, told Mike, "You have to differentiate yourself, your products, your services from everyone else. You must continue to explore new markets for your existing products in the globalized business world. And above all, be people-driven, because motivated people are the ones who grow a business." G.E. Capital's success and growth is a validation of this philosophy.

Warning sign #7: Leadership changes frequently. Continuity at the top gives people some assurance that the game plan won't be changed capriciously. The pattern of continuous reorganizing, reengineering and downsizing has caused dramatic discontent among workers all over the world, especially in the U.S. When leaders are caught in this shuffle, shock waves roll through the company.

Stable leadership from the CEO and all of the top executives (all of whom are likely to have huge followings among the rank and file) is a must. When leadership changes frequently, the fabric of an organization is torn apart, and productivity, quality and creativity suffer.

Solution: Build organizations with enough stability to ensure loyalty among the employees. Don't displace the captain of the ship every time there's a storm on the horizon.

Manage by constructive values rather than just worshipping the bottom line. (This will be discussed in detail in Chapter 10.)

What is a creative climate?

A creative climate is an atmosphere for achievement. A creative climate encourages everyone to come up with something new—something that works. Things get done, ideas get implemented.

As Buckminster Fuller observed, the universe itself is fundamentally creative. People are continually discovering new things about themselves—their talents, their capacities, their outlooks. And they also keep discovering new things about the cosmos—new solar systems, new galaxies and even new principles about the fundamental nature of their world.

Creativity is ongoing. It's everywhere you look. Just consider spring following winter, year after year. Consider natural wonders like the Grand Canyon.

Creativity is in nature. It's in everything you do, see or think. Creativity is the motor of the universe! Creativity is also your motor.

Creativity is the prime motivating force, waiting for you to tap into its potential. Our friend George Fink once said, "Creativity is everything. It's why I live."

Creativity is not purely inherent

A few people believe that creativity is a purely inherent talent found only in certain people. Contrary to that belief, creativity is both inherent and learned. One of the ways you establish a creative climate is by helping people let go of their hang-ups and assisting them in understanding operating principles. One way to tap into the creative process is to take advantage of a predetermined method for creative thinking, such as the various systems that we teach.

Creativity is not the opposite of organization

There are companies that set aside special days for their employees to be creative. This may be a step in the right direction, but it doesn't help people grasp the nature of creativity.

The schedule shouldn't be interrupted to make room for creativity. It should embrace and support creativity as an intrinsic activity!

Creativity should be an open, liberating, unstructured aspect of work, but it should be included as part of organized time. Creative thinking can also be organized outside of the normal routine, of course, but if you don't build creativity into the very fabric of what you do, you've missed establishing a culture in which the opportunities for breakthroughs abound.

Walt Disney didn't set aside a period for "creative work"—as distinguished from other work—to be undertaken on Mondays, Wednesdays and Fridays between the hours of 3 and 5 p.m. He built creativity into the culture of his company, and he did it in an organized way. Walt understood, and made a point of telling anyone in his company who would listen, that contrary to popular belief, creativity flourishes in the best organized environments.

"Organized" is not to be mistaken for "perpetually controlling." The more organized the environment, the more organized people's work habits, the more organized the culture. And the more organized the culture, the more time people will have to engage in effective creative thinking that can produce outstanding results.

There are companies that think they can't afford to take the time to implement creativity into their cultures. They think they can't afford to develop a workplace that constantly reinforces creativity. But if they analyzed the potential benefits of establishing a creative culture compared with the costs of their current ways of doing business, they would conclude that they can't afford not to take steps to incorporate creativity into their culture.

Creativity is not the absence of planning. We were working with a company president not long ago who said, in essence, "Making it up as we go along is our corporate culture! That's how we operate! We plan on the fly in between meetings."

Such companies may call their working environments "creative," but they are, in fact, extraordinarily stressful, wasteful and noncreative places to work. This type of chaotic "culture" costs organizations untold millions of dollars a year. We can't even estimate the loss of creativity.

Creativity is the cause. Productivity is the effect. Companies invest heavily in training programs for productivity and reengineering, hoping to learn how to assure success in a particular, narrowly focused area. They should focus on ways to establish a creative climate on the personal and organizational level.

Creativity's biggest obstacle: uptight people

We've studied creativity for years in an attempt to understand it and get in tune with those techniques that bring about greater levels of creativity. One of the most important discoveries we've made in working with our clients during project planning, idea development and implementation is that there is a very common, very correctable obstacle most companies face in addressing the issue of creativity.

The biggest obstacle to a creative climate is that too many people tend to be uptight and rigid. Creativity means opening up to possibilities. And yet most companies encourage their employees to shut down rather than open up. People should ask, "What could happen if we tried this?" Answering this question requires a mind freed from preconceptions, a mind that can open up like a flower. People have to let go, for at least a moment. But most won't let go for five seconds! They're holding everything in! What they need is a "creativity laxative"! You can't possibly have a creative climate when people in the organization can't stop clenching their teeth for more than 10 minutes at a stretch, much less an hour. Most people have been trained not to have fun at work. Not to be playful. Not to let go and be spontaneous.

When people hold back and deny how they feel about something, they're not open to the conditions of the moment, and they tend to be neurotic. They don't free their feelings. Because of this, problem-solving in business and government is often neurotic instead of creative.

There are many steps you can take to initiate a creative climate, but none of them will work if you don't first let go of habits that put you in the box!

Ways to let go and break out of the box

Change your setting

Sometimes the first step in letting go is the simple act of getting out of the building.

People need to get out of the high rise, office park or home office in order to stop looking at the same four walls where they spend all day fighting the battle and pushing themselves. (One way to get away is to attend our Break Out of the Box seminars and tailored workshops.)

They need to do something, anything besides have another meeting in which they try to "come up with a creative solution" to a particular problem... under an impossible deadline.

Companies get into a problem situation, a slow-down period, and everyone is told, "We need to cut back; we need to get more creative and make do with less. And we need your recommendations by Monday morning at 8:30 a.m."

Solutions that arise from this mind-set usually aren't the best. These demands make people more uptight at exactly the wrong time. At this point, laxatives don't even work; people need a creativity proctologist!

Indulge in five-sensing

We deal with five-sensing in our book *Think Out of the Box*, where we coined a word that describes five-sensory exploration: *sensanation.*

This means learning to think in all five senses—sight, smell, touch, taste and hearing—rather than just one sense. Typically, people use the sense of sight by visualizing solutions through a process called imagination (image-ination), the formation of mental images. But this isn't the only way to be creative. If you truly let go, all five senses get a workout.

The last time we worked with Buckminster Fuller, he exemplified this concept in his use of his sense of hearing (and his sense of humor).

We had arranged a photo shoot with Fuller. The cameraman was clicking off pictures. Click, click, click! After a few shots, the photographer reminded us that we all needed to smile before we heard the click. Fuller said, "What we need is a 'pre-click' camera!" And today many cameras do make such a warning sound before they expose film. We like to think that Bucky helped that cameraman develop the first prototype.

For the rest of the shoot, the photographer said, "Click!" Then we would smile—quite genuinely—and the photographer would hit the button. Click!

When you are open to experiencing a situation, when you use your senses to their fullest, the result is spontaneity and an ability to combine the old with the new.

Let's think about each of the major senses, starting with vision.

Seeing things clearly

Opening your sense of sight means increasing your perspective by making an effort to see the entirety of the world around you, not just the tiny chunk that happens to boot up on your laptop. It means expanding your parameters until you see something remarkable, something unexpected. This is called "seeing the big picture."

Corporate workplaces rarely expose their employees to exciting visual stimuli. You can change this! In your own work area—and in common areas to the degree you're allowed—you should make an effort to keep some form of beauty around. The beauty can be simple or complex, but as long as it's aesthetically pleasing to you, it's worth incorporating. For example, place a small aquarium with exotic fish in common areas. Put up posters of fine art. Bring huge, dramatic plants into the office.

Another way to maximize your sense of sight is to try to find beauty that's already present, either in the workplace or elsewhere. We find that changing settings (or routines) can be a big help on this score. Think of a dark night at the top of the mountain, with just a few stars twinkling an eternity or two away. Or think of a magnificent sunny day in a park where people are walking, music is playing and children are running.

Open up to the beauty around you. What will you see? Perhaps you'll see the innocence in the face of a child—or the life in the face of a person who's 90. That's beautiful!

You can push your sense of sight to its highest point by using travel—virtual or actual—to find exciting new forms of stimulus. Today, "travel" can mean an actual cruise, a stunning public television documentary or even a trip around the world on the World Wide Web. Real-life experiences are probably the best way to go, but the other activities can be mind-opening as well.

Chase down a rainbow. Maybe you can find one by looking out your kitchen window. Or take a helicopter ride on the Hawaiian island of Maui. Rainbows are all over the place there. Don't pass by a rainbow without looking and feeling it! Natural creativity is everywhere. Find as many ways as possible to acknowledge and embrace it in your own life.

There's a hilltop in Bangladesh where you can look out at a seemingly endless line of bushes with fireflies on nearly every leaf. They're called synchronous fireflies. Talk about awesome beauty! You look down at miles of bushes where there are hundred of fireflies—all blinking on and off simultaneously. Sometimes they'll fill a whole tree, and you can stand there and watch the tree go on and off like a neon sign. There are a lot of theories about the phenomenon—nobody's really sure how the fireflies manage to blink on and off in harmony. But they do it!

If you're interested in generating a breathtaking moment, in exposing yourself to an awesome stimulus, the wonders in nature are capable of revealing beauty that is unsurpassed. Someday, you may want to take the opportunity to experience the synchronous fireflies with someone you love. Or maybe you'll find something even more wondrous to look at, something that's closer to home.

The sound of music

Do you remember the movie *The Music Man?* The central character, professor Harold Hill, always heard the band, even when it wasn't around. We want people to hear that band playing in their ears and in their hearts. There is an instruction from a meditation course: Be calm, be quiet, be open and hear the music of the morning and of the evening.

It's easy to tune sounds out. It takes an effort to hear the music, to feel its vibrations. When you listen, you enter a world of infinite possibilities. There is inspiration when you keep the channels open and hear the band.

Think of a big city during rush hour. Amid the noise and clatter of the city, if someone flung a silver dollar into the air, perhaps 100 people would hear that silver dollar hit the ground. Most of us tend to be money-oriented rather than experience-oriented. How many of us would hear a tiny cricket chirping away in the bush right next to the spot where the dollar fell?

A taste of inspiration

It's really difficult to think about taste. You have to taste taste.

Let go! Why not taste all the flavors you can in a single day? How about some espresso or delicious cappuccino? How about a tangy margarita? Get out there and for one day really blow it! Tackle a big chocolate chip cookie-dough ice cream cone.

Slow down your eating habits to enjoy the act of tasting. Savor the flavor of foods that you're supposed to pass up. You lose out on pleasure by inhaling your food. One way to let go is to eat, drink and be merry—once in a while at any rate. Don't worry about it. Just do it if your health permits. See what happens. You may be able to justify this so-called "excess" by rekindling your zest and passion for life. Experience your sense of taste. Come alive!

And remember the famous toast often given at banquets before downing something exhilarating. *"À votre santé!"* To your health!

The touch of creativity

Touching remains one of the most intimate of the senses. It creates a feeling that no other sense can communicate.

Leo Buscaglia encouraged people to find people they love and give them a great big hug when they least expect it. It's sad that in today's litigious culture you probably can't hug someone spontaneously in the workplace.

Dr. Ashley Montague, the famed anthropologist, called touch "cutaneous stimulation." He pointed out that babies die when they don't get touched regularly. Grown-ups die from lack of touching, too, but at a slower pace.

The smell of new ideas

The sense of smell is often unappreciated, because people have been culturally conditioned to tune out or cover up natural smells. It's a phenomenon partly explained by the fact that people try to eliminate bad smells or offensive odors. The adjective "stuck up" originally referred to people who raised their noses and tried to block out repugnant aromas.

The engineering genius inherent in the sense of smell is fantastic. Smell can warn of impending dangers lurking in a toxic gas or a smoldering fire. It can summon up memories.

Many smells simply go unnoticed, thanks to a socially reinforced practice of sensory denial that becomes a habit. There are individuals who smell bad to those outside their cultural group, but are perfectly acceptable to those within their group. Nongarlic eaters have a real problem with those who make a habit of eating cloves of raw garlic.

Cultivating an appreciation for smell usually requires extra effort and thoughtfulness. In our seminars, we place a lot of emphasis on using smells in a positive, creativity-enhancing way by putting scented candles on display tables. We also put scented candles in our offices and homes. (Brandon Toropov, a writer we know, only gets down to business at his laptop after he's lit a cone of Spiritual Sky incense.) Scented candles can trigger thoughts and memories that lead to inspiration, causing us to look at a situation differently.

Use your senses to break out!

You can use your sensory perceptions to help you break out of the box. Change your settings by enriching the sensory input. Change your stimulus!

Change the input and you'll change the output.

Helen Keller, who was blind and deaf, reportedly developed her sense of smell so keenly that she was able to steer a canoe down the middle of a stream by smelling the foliage on either side of the stream. This is what we mean by "being open to the experience"!

Can you stimulate all five senses at once? Yes! It happens all the time. If you've ever gone to Palm Springs, California, in the spring, you know it's a magnificent time when the date trees are in bloom. In the early morning, when people are watering the dates and the sun is just coming up, you can walk through the spray and breathe in the fabulous fragrance. The sight of the desert sun, the sound of falling water, the scent of fresh dates, the feel of water rolling down you, the taste of water on your lips. Suddenly you're surrounded by new envelopes of natural sights, scents, sounds, sensations and tastes.

It happens everywhere. It happens all the time. You don't even have to go to Palm Springs. (Although it's certainly nice if you can!)

Start with one sense. Pushing one sense to the limit often causes the rest to follow. Do whatever it takes, but find some way to let go. Which sense will you choose? Maybe it's taste. Go for it! Blow your diet on an occasional high-calorie malted milkshake, if your health permits. Start a mini revolution. Push one of your senses to the limit! Show the world who's boss.

Diets. Meetings. Deadlines. Jobs. We're not saying these things are somehow unnecessary. They're fine, and they are part of our lives. At the same time, however, one of the reasons people fall into the anticreativity mode is that they get into a pattern they pursue so long and so hard that they become boxed in.

If you're going to break out of the box, you must be willing to let go of the standard pattern for a moment. Doing something unusual with one or more of your senses is a proven way to accomplish this.

Once Mike was in Mexico conducting a seminar for the Centro Nacional de Productividad on creative thinking techniques. The setting was the Hotel Jurica near the small mission town of Queretaro. It turned out to be a magnificent experience because of the exotic sensory stimuli.

He walked out into the courtyard of Hotel Jurica, where tropical birds of every color were singing at the top of their lungs. The music was beautiful. Before breakfast, an unsaddled horse was tied up outside his suite, ready for him to ride.

The riding trail began at an aqueduct that brought water right out of the hills to the hotel. Water would drip down through huge arches as Mike rode his horse in and out of each arch. He could hear the sounds of the dripping water; he could taste it falling on his mouth; he could feel its coldness on his body. Lovely bougainvillea bushes trailed down the aqueduct's stone pillars, giving off a sweet fragrance Mike would never forget.

He rode back watching the sunrise over the Mexican horizon. When he got back to the hotel, he enjoyed a five-star breakfast, served to the sound of a *mariachi* band. A beautiful *señorita* dressed in a blue silk shawl with bougainvillea blossoms in her hair served the meal.

85

It was an amazing experience, one that opened Mike up to a new world of possibilities. We all need more experiences like that.

Plan vicarious experiences

Mike directed teenage camps in Ohio and California for a number of years. When he began this career, he didn't realize that his job was to keep the kids inside the camp. Before long, he realized that this meant that the camp would have to be interesting and truly creative if he was going to keep the campers there of their own volition.

He set up "vicarious experience" days. On such a day, one camper would, for example, wear a blindfold and have to make it through the day's activities without benefit of sight. Another person would guide the blindfolded camp member everywhere he or she went. This exercise allowed the participants to embrace more fully those senses they had and to appreciate the gift of sight once the blindfold came off.

But it was more than a sensory exercise. It was a relationship exercise, as well. Mike would wake up at 6 a.m., blindfold 10 people, then assign 10 more people as guides. For this task, he'd always pick people who needed to develop a little more sensitivity to the feelings of others. The blindfolded campers would usually develop a healthy respect for their four other major senses. The guides would usually learn to look at the world in a less self-centered way.

There were other variations. Sometimes Mike would select people who had to remain silent all day. (Talk about a challenge! We are the first to admit that, for us, this would probably be one of the hardest vicarious experiences.) When these people would say their first word of the day at the end of the evening, they'd have a new perspective on the simple joy of speaking. They'd have a new way of experiencing things, and that's a necessary precursor of initiating personal and organizational breakthroughs.

Other people—again, usually those who had a feeling that the world revolved around them—had their hands tied behind their backs. Suddenly, they realized an important fact about the world: Everyone has to rely on another person in some way. For them, on that day, this experience was very direct. They needed help to get food, open doors, manage difficult pathways where the bush intruded and so on. At the same time, someone else had to give in completely, had to learn to think in a more inclusive way. This type of thinking moves beyond "How does this affect me?" to "How does this affect us?" Any task requiring any kind of physical manipulation quickly became a two-person operation. So much for the myth of complete self-sufficiency!

These exercises not only developed greater sensitivity toward people who face physical challenges but helped those involved on both sides of these activities to become more fully aware of themselves as human beings. Mike wanted to help them to let go of the illusory notion that people always have complete control over the situations they face. True control, the campers learned, arises more out of adaptability and participation than out of preprogrammed responses.

A technique we have used to teach the importance of adaptability and participation involved the pairing of two unlikely partners: a top executive and a baby. Talk about fun!

Six wingtip-friendly CEOs showed up at the pool. There, waiting for them, were six borrowed babies, each between 6 months and 1 year old, and all non-swimmers. First, we reviewed the fairly simple process of teaching infants to swim. Inevitably, there were some CEOs who wanted to take their own approach: Toss 'em in and let them go for it on their own! (These are usually the people who have the most to learn about participative management.) Others tried to master every rule and even got competitive with the others: "I've got it all down. My baby will learn to swim faster than your baby!" Babies aren't actually that predictable. The day's activities always had a way of teaching the CEOs some important lessons about humility.

Instilling a creative company culture

A creative climate is established by doing whatever you can with your current environment to shift your outlook. The material and resources you need to do this are actually all around you. The challenge is recognizing them. The organization's culture and physical surroundings should help foster the recognition of these resources.

A healthy and constructive culture has become the key to successful company growth. The current emphasis on improving culture is not a passing fad, but a major new thrust that is becoming a national movement. Competitive survival in today's business world depends on maintaining rich cultures that routinely stimulate people to be original thinkers, to ask: What would Walt Disney do? What would Leonardo da Vinci do? What would Thomas Edison do?

More and more, companies are building environments where people are encouraged to ask, "How would so-and-so tackle this particular problem?"

This type of original thinking gives people a true competitive advantage. It takes time to develop and nurture, but it is what helps create unique products and services.

Throughout recorded history, successful cultures have been the result of original thinking. Anything that promotes original thinking, such as encouraging people to break out of their personal boxes by using sensory stimuli in the ways we've discussed, helps to foster a creative culture.

Those cultures that engage in the most original thinking leave behind the richest legacies.

If original thinking diminishes, if the environment becomes unfavorable to original thinking, the culture begins to die. Then other cultures (perhaps those of an organization's competitors) will emerge and dominate.

People require time to become acclimated to a culture. Who hasn't heard the term "culture shock"? Someone who's spent 25 years in Bangladesh wouldn't be expected to make a successful overnight transition to life in Manhattan. People who are moving from one way of working to another need time to adjust.

A sensitivity to those entering and trying to make sense of a new work environment is an essential part of developing a rich and successful culture. The culture is strongest when it helps veterans deliver breakthrough thinking but also offers entry points for newcomers. Even small companies with limited resources should find a way to address cultural issues.

At organizations large and small, team members should find ways to address financial constraints together. Look at the issues as a team, and you'll find the know-how. Even though it may sound as though it should curtail creativity, limiting resources and making do with what's available is sometimes the very best way to encourage breakthroughs.

In 1962, a new group called the Beatles, by no means a proven commodity, were allotted one day of EMI's studio time to complete 10 new songs for their first British album. Schedules and budgets would permit the newcomers no more time than that.

In a little more than 10 hours, the group had recorded an album that would spend more than half a year at the top of the English charts—and launch perhaps the most extraordinary show business career in history. That's called getting the most out of your resources!

In the right culture, limited resources can stimulate rather than inhibit group thinking and achievement. A breakthrough!

You also must respond to the needs of the group, not make them respond to you. Dr. Maria Montessori, the famed education reformer, spoke of identifying and reacting appropriately to "the teaching moment"—that moment when a student's mind is open. Responding appropriately to the teaching moment is a very different task than force-feeding facts!

Spotting and taking advantage of this teaching opportunity is an essential skill that is worth mastering if you hope to help others grow in their ability.

The long term

Cultures, of course, do not happen overnight. They evolve. Developing a culture is an ongoing process, one that must be encouraged and nurtured by careful planning. You may want the results as soon as possible, but what are you willing to do to help bring them about over time?

What is going to happen next month, next quarter, next year to help instill the organization's culture?

In working to help companies plan and develop unique corporate cultures, we find that, often, corporate leaders don't analyze where they are at the beginning of the process. They don't take the time to describe what the current culture is. An organization can't get somewhere later if its leaders don't know where it is now! (For more details on this subject, listen to our audiocassette *Cultivating Company Cultures.*)

You must know where you stand now. Then you can think about where you want to be, what kind of culture you want to implement and why. Once you know where you are, you can consider the new features that you can put into the plan to encourage a new way of thinking. If you fail to take account of your current situation, the new culture will not endure.

New cultures fade away rapidly when the foundation is not constructed carefully. Often, as companies grow, the early results of a new culture are effective, but later, during growth periods, that culture is diluted. Why? The company doesn't have a handle on the basics of either the old culture or the new one, and the old ways of operating reappear. That's when the CEO asks us, "What happened to our participative culture?"

What happened to it? No one watched it. No one watered it. No one nurtured it. No one cared. People must be involved, informed and inspired. That means devoting time, attention and energy to the maintenance of the culture!

In organizations large and small, there should be a person and/or department trained to be in charge of supporting the company's culture.

What makes a culture?

Here are some areas in which you can nurture distinctive approaches that will help you establish (or reestablish) a creative culture in your workplace.

1. Your special traditions. What is it that your company has always rewarded or regarded highly? What standards have you upheld consistently? What standards should you uphold consistently? Develop cultural traditions that reflect these standards.

2. Your rituals. What routines and ceremonies does your company follow that are different from those of any other organization? What rituals make your organization unique! Develop cultural differentiators.

3. Your symbols and language. What logos, terminology or ways of communicating set you apart from the rest of the pack—and help inspire people to high levels of achievement?

4. Your special ways of celebrating victories. How do you celebrate achievement? And do you celebrate achievement? Be sure that a unique social event appropriate to the occasion accompanies the victories your people rack up.

5. Your work habits. What time do people show up for, and leave from, work? What is the outlook on occasional variations from these standards? How do people work? Must they always work that way? Some companies look at such issues rigidly, and tolerate few deviations from established procedures. Others are more flexible.

6. Your workspaces. Do you have open spaces? Are the look and feel of work areas prescribed or can individuals adapt them to reflect personal style? For a full discussion of the physical aspects of the creative work environment, see the following, as well as the discussion of participatory workspaces in Chapter 8.

More about workspaces

The Team Center is one of the most exciting, fastest-growing concepts in the business world today.

A Team Center is a resource-rich working environment that reshapes the way a company operates. There is also a counterpart for the individual working at home, which we call A Kitchen for the Mind; this environment is discussed in our book, *Think Out of the Box*, and in our audiocassette series *A Creative Living Center: A Kitchen for the Mind*.

The Team Center is effective for work groups because it can be adapted to any company of any size. The objective is to set aside one space that will serve as your Team Center, and equip it with Displayed Thinking boards around all the walls of the space for high visual impact.

With Displayed Thinking, concepts and ideas surround you as you walk into the room, allowing you to encounter issues in a highly visualized way. Images related to projects and problems that the team is working on are visible to everyone.

The Team Center will also include the technology the team will be using—typically in a line of desks or tabletops that runs down the center of the room. Think of the system the room represents. Consider the room to be like the software for the hardware within a computer, or like the engine in a car.

Quick and easy steps for building a Team Center

1. Select a room.

2. Cover the walls with visual stimuli, so that everywhere you look some visual element of the project meets your eyes. In hotel ballrooms, we often use huge 4' x 8' pinnable boards that can be leaned up against a wall. These boards become part of the working environment. They should be well-lit, easy to read and equipped with plenty of blank cards so your team can add or rearrange ideas as the situation demands.

3. Add the technology you'll use for interaction—computers, printers and typewriters. All of it can run right down the middle of the room. No compartments! No cubicles! No doors! No obstacles!

Wall-to-wall high visualization means you're immersed in the project. Centrally located technology means easy access back and forth to the computer from the Displayed Thinking walls. The Team Center environment needs to be flexible. In a Team Center, everyone can see the scope of the project in its totality!

Making your Team Center work

Keep the information on the Displayed Thinking boards simple and direct, and make it visually arresting. (Particularly complex information or confidential materials can be coded or stored in a secure computer database.)

Remember that the Team Center creates an "eyes-on" experience. Everyone involved must be immersed in the "big picture." This visual emphasis triggers involvement and inspiration through utilization of the S-P-R sequence. This stands for Stimulus (the visual element around which the team congregates), Pause (when a team conducts research and development on a project) and Response (the new initiative or idea that arises from the Pause).

The Team Center immerses people immediately in the work at hand! It surrounds them with visual project-related stimulation and provides them with technological resources at the core of the room.

Dramatic results

Team Centers dramatically enhance the creativity and efficiency of work groups. They help work groups make the most of the strengths of their technologies and even compensate for the weaknesses of the technologies by making them less dehumanizing and antisocial.

The Team Center's focus is on people and creative thinking techniques, not machines. Think of the Team Center as a resource-rich environment where the tools are brought together in a way that permits everyone to make contributions and solve problems. This room is similar to a kitchen: Everything you need for the recipe is at your fingertips.

Still another way to think of the Team Center is as a lake or a pond where you're going fishing for big ideas. The walls are the edges of the lake. When you put up Displayed Thinking boards or project-related cards, as well as other visual input, those cards are like the lures that you throw into the water. You're trying to find where the big fish are!

This is exactly what Walt Disney did in his team units at the Disney studio. He and his people were fishing for big ideas—trophy fish. The more lures you have to throw, the better the chance you have for landing the big one.

> *"The answer's out there—if you're looking for it."*
> —Thomas Edison

If you're not looking for it, if you're not fishing, if you're not putting anything into the water, what's going to happen? You're not going to catch any fish!

Team Centers build involvement

It often happens that executives call us and say, "We have a major problem. We can't solve it. We need your help!"

We always ask, "Well, who's working on it?" And the answer comes back: "Nobody."

We ask, "Why?" The answer: "Because we can't solve it!"

If no one is working on a problem, it can't be solved. That's a major point!

One of the benefits of the Team Center environment is that it dramatically encourages involvement in the issue of the day. It's participative. It's also energizing; it turns average meetings into creative, breakthrough sessions. It helps build, reinforce and support a strong creative culture!

Does the Team Center work by itself? No. It needs a methodology, a guiding hand, a series of choices and events regarding organization and attack. That's where the breakthrough facilitator comes in. That's where the methodology of our Creative Thinking Techniques, detailed in Chapter 6 of our book, *Think Out of the Box*, come in.

By the same token, if organizations try to execute a new plan in the same old stultifying, cookie-cutter cubicles—or send people one message about the value of their input on paper but an opposite message in their working environments—then the plan won't take off.

Remember: Your environment produces your experiences. Your experiences stimulate your convictions and opinions, and these convictions, in turn, help to reinforce values. Values are the ideas in which you really do believe and for which you are willing to take action.

The dynamic culture, the culture that really works, is the culture in which people are willing to put values into action.

Summary

➤ There are seven warning signs that an existing culture needs to be changed:

1. People are having difficulty accepting new ideas and adopting new technologies. They are resisting change. (Use participation to involve people in the creation of new ideas!)

2. People are bogged down in routine and fixed procedures. (Review the routines and change what needs to be changed!)

3. Poor ideas are being generated. ("Court" the ideas for longer periods of time before finalizing them!)

4. Excessive politicking is taking place. (Get people off of the sidelines and into the game!)

5. Few ideas are being implemented. (Grant people more authority!)

6. Philosophies and products are becoming outdated. (Embrace realistic expansion plans and dynamic change!)

7. Leadership changes frequently. (Ride out the storm. Manage by constructive values rather than just worshipping the bottom line.)

➢ A creative climate is an atmosphere for achievement.

➢ Creativity is not a purely inherent process, nor is it the opposite of organization.

➢ The biggest obstacle to creativity is uptight people.

➢ Use "five-sensing" to open up to the beauty of the world around you, and to find out more about yourself. (This is a great tool for breaking out of the box.)

➢ Company cultures are recognized as a composite of values, standards and goals.

➢ Even though it may sound as though it should curtail creativity, limiting resources and making do with what's available is sometimes the very best way to encourage breakthroughs.

➢ Consider incorporating a Team Center into your work environment to foster a truly creative culture! Team Centers build involvement and deliver dramatic results!

Profile: Encouraging a Creative Climate

Walter E. Disney
Roy O. Disney

The Disney Brothers
Founders, The Walt Disney Company

In many ways, the Disney brothers, Walt and Roy, were like all brothers. They agreed and disagreed, they argued and debated, they fought and made up. But from another point of view the Disney brothers were also unlike most other sets of brothers, because out of their struggle came one of the greatest entertainment empires in human history, an organization that has left its mark on society in a unique way. The company the two men built represents the highest mark of combined fraternal achievement, the goal to aim for in any partnership.

Other famous brothers were behind airplanes, medical clinics, cough drops, automobiles, gunfighting legends and even another motion picture studio just down the street from the one the Disneys built. However, none of those brothers captivated the imagination of the world solely with ink, paint, pens, pencils and a special approach known as Imagineering. These two brothers from Kansas were pioneers who understood how to break out of the box. They built creative climates that gave birth to originality in entertainment.

Mike has found that people around the world are fascinated by and generally interested in learning exactly how the brothers did it. He has a unique perspective on this, having studied them firsthand for more than seven years as head of management development and dean of Disney University.

Mike's office and team units were just across the hall from Walt, and quite near Roy. He spent many hours discussing the brothers and their working relationship with those who helped them build the Disney company, and his research projects brought Mike many opportunities to see how both of them worked together. He has several hundred pages of notes taken during the years that he worked at Disney.

Fact or fiction

There has been much written about these two legendary brothers that is inaccurate or distorted by individuals who never met them or worked with them. Also, it's important to remember that, among Disney's closest colleagues, certain stories became sacrosanct, perhaps even apocryphal, as the company culture grew and developed over the years.

A case in point is the revealing story of how Walt got his inspiration for starting Disneyland by taking his daughters, Sharon and Diane, to the Carousel at Griffith Park in Los Angeles. Instructors told this story in courses at Disney University, but Mike never heard the full version of it from Walt himself. He heard aspects of it told by Roy at various dinners throughout the years. Nevertheless, it remains Mike's favorite example of how Walt's mind worked, how he looked at things and how he could develop a vision out of almost anything.

As Mike heard it, Walt considered Saturday to be what he called "Daddy's Day" with his two daughters. He would often take them to Griffith Park in Los Angeles for an outing. The park was large and contained many attractions that children loved. There was a pony ride and a miniature train ride, followed by "Train Town," which housed a collection of old trains and locomotives. Kids could board them and fantasize about being the conductor of the grand machines. But the biggest attraction of all was a magnificent old carousel set atop a hill.

Walt would put his girls on the carousel and sit on a bench holding their popcorn and candy while he watched them ride around and around. He said the popcorn was stale, the cotton candy was limp and the employees at the carousel couldn't care less if the patrons were there. Making matters even worse, he noticed the horses on the carousel were all supposed to be jumpers, but that some of them didn't go up and down. What's more, the paint on the carousel horses was badly chipped and peeling away in many places. Needless to say, this bothered Walt very much. It bothered him enough to make him pick up his sketchpad and pencil to begin drawing.

He began to sketch out ideas that would later become Disneyland. He said, "I wanted to create a place where a daddy could go and have as much fun as his little girls and boys. Just imagine if you're a little girl, looking forward all week to taking a trip to the park with your dad, and you get on a horse that won't jump. That's awful. Add to this chipped paint, stale popcorn, limp cotton candy and unpleasant employees. What a disappointment."

At Disney University, this was the beginning of the mission statement: "A place where all the horses jump and there's no chipped paint." Instructors then told the story about Walt taking his daughters to the park on Saturday. The carousel itself became the symbol of the mission.

Later, when Mike started his own company to assist others to break out of the box by creating dynamic cultures, he used the carousel concept to make the mission fun and exciting. In fact, this idea of making the mission fun rather than drudgery became the starting point of the personal computer revolution. A.C. (Mike) Markkula, Apple's cofounder, acknowledged that this was the genesis of Apple Values and the runaway spirit unleashed in Silicon Valley. He said, "One of the lessons from Disney was: We're on an adventure together. Apple isn't supposed to be drudgery."

Jim Burke at AT&T also used this culture-building concept. He and others told AT&T staff the story of the carousel. Then they related it to providing exceptional service to AT&T's customers. Jim had a beautiful pin made of a golden horse from the carousel to give for outstanding service performance. They presented it with a picture of the actual carousel at Griffith Park. So Walt's experience at the carousel even influenced a culture tradition in this group at AT&T.

Walt taught these three principles for building a company culture:

1. **A statement:** Put your mission or vision into a clear, simple and succinct statement. It is most powerful when the statement relates to an actual experience.

2. **A story:** Tell a story that explains the statement of your mission or vision. If it is a true story, it is more motivating to people.

3. **A symbol:** Symbols are ideas made visible. Try to create a symbol or logo that reflects the story and the mission statement. It is helpful to render this symbol in a picture or pin.

Mike reviewed this entire concept to a convention of one of the nation's largest fast-food chains. The company's president approached him at the swimming pool of the Maui Hyatt with his company's operation manual. Mike had told the convention the carousel story, putting emphasis on "all horses jump" and "no chipped paint."

The food chain's president opened the manual to the first page and read to Mike the contents of a box on the page. The box said: "It is our philosophy to wash all windows in our stores the minute they get dirty. The same principle will be applied to everything else and embodies our operating philosophy."

The president said, "You see, we also follow Walt Disney's philosophy in our company."

Mike said, "No, that's the opposite of Walt Disney's philosophy. His philosophy was that the windows don't get dirty. Clean them even before they are dirty. This is a totally different concept."

Original thinking

Walt and Roy were original thinkers. Walt was an artistic genius with an understanding of the financial, Roy was a financial genius with an understanding of the artistic. This resulted in a unique brand of give-and-take that led to original solutions and unique approaches to problems.

Walt had very specific views and opinions on just what produced original ideas. He expressed those beliefs to those around him without hesitation. Here, collected from Mike's notes and recollections, are nine of the most important views.

Walt's views on original thinking

1. **Avoid trite jargon and clichés.** Banalities, bromides and platitudes often become a substitute for really thinking a problem through. Walt felt that buzzwords and clichés often make us think something is happening when it isn't.

2. **Don't copy, steal or plagiarize.** Respect the intellectual property of others and expect the same in return. Walt had felt the sting of having one of his first characters, Oswald the Rabbit, stolen right out from under him. He never forgot this transgression, and thereafter aggressively pursued those who infringed on Disney's copyrights and trademarks.

3. **Ask probing questions.** Go to the core of a problem or task by doing good R&D. Walt said, "When we start a project, we really study it from every angle. We literally walk around it from every point of view in order to leave no stone unturned."

4. **Use stories to communicate.** Walt was probably one of the premier storytellers of our time. He was a raconteur without equal who could regale his listeners for hours without ever boring them.

5. **Remember that the best answers are often the simplest answers.** Original thinking is blocked by making a task or challenge too complex. The complicated or Byzantine didn't ever cloud Walt's thinking or creativity. He said, "Keep it so simple a child can understand it."

6. **Be a nonconformist.** Walt believed that breaking out of the box required being a nonconformist. He had a respect for tradition, laws, manners and decency, but he was willing to explore new approaches that might go against other people's cherished preconceptions.

7. **Avoid sequels.** He hated repeating last year's success but loved breaking new ground. He believed that sequels weaken your creative muscle by becoming a crutch to lean on when you can't come up with something original.

8. **Study creativity in nature.** Walt, like many other highly creative people, studied and observed creativity in nature. He said, "I like to watch animals to find clues as to how old Mother Nature handles a problem. Some people just get too busy with scripts, payrolls and bankers to smell the flowers. I've done it myself, and our originality suffered."

9. **Find connections between things.** Walt said, "One thing leads to another thing. It's important to find the connections between the parts if we expect to come up with original solutions. Put the ideas up on a board to help you see the connections." He would often say, "Show it to me. Don't tell it to me."

Roy's rules for executives

Roy Disney and his wife Edna often ate dinner at the Smoke House Restaurant, where Mike and others held many dinners and discussions for the management development programs. One evening, the group gathered informally around Roy's table and discussed his rules for guiding managers or executives. These were spontaneous, off-the-cuff observations from Roy that we have continued to use in our work.

1. **Stay knowledgeable about developing technologies.** Roy Disney, even in his 70s, was up on developing technology. He told Mike to include the subject in Disney's management development programs by inviting guest lecturers on advanced technology concepts to speak to the groups. He said, "It's our responsibility to know what technology is available to us right now, and what is being created in R&D labs around the world."

2. **List those about to emerge.** Roy felt it was not enough just to know what technologies there were. It was important to actually make a list of them with the possible applications in your area of expertise. He really pinned down the technology issue to specifics rather than vague generalities. For example, Roy might ask: "What direction will the computer take? How will it affect managing a theme park and movie studio? What advanced technology will help us automate through the use of robotics?"

3. **Pick a technology wave to ride.** Roy wanted managers and executives to take some risks on technology trends they believed in. He said, "Pick a technology that you will bet on and believe in because of the research you've given to the subject. Convince all of us that we should join with you."

4. **Don't be premature (or late) in picking your technology.** This admonition should make us be careful about our conclusions, and help us to avoid being taken for a ride by overzealous promoters.

5. **Keep personal skills in synch with physical technology.** Roy didn't want machines to replace people or displace them into secondary roles. He saw them only as a kind of support that would increase individual productivity.

6. **Go beyond money.** Roy once told us this story: "A big investment banker called the other day to say he wanted to invest some big money in our Orlando project. He said that he would give us practically anything we want. I said that money was easy to get. What we need is investors who will also make a contribution to the project. Get people to bring ideas along with their money."

Borrowed Heroes

The Disney brothers were not publicity hounds or glory seekers. They were essentially low-key individuals who established creative climates for their employees. Walt often said, "We don't have any geniuses around here. We're all in the same boat, and we are only as good as our next picture."

He and Roy didn't want to be considered heroes in their own company. One morning in an elevator, Walt told Mike in no uncertain terms: "Don't go and make me a hero in your training programs. This puts everyone else on a lower notch. I don't like that or believe that. We've got a lot of artists around here, a lot of directors and producers and a lot of leaders. You make me the hero and it makes 'em mad inside. Let's have a borrowed hero, someone like da Vinci."

Thus the Borrowed Hero concept was born. If you think it through, this concept makes a lot of sense, especially in trying to encourage teamwork in an organization.

We have encouraged our clients to try this approach in building their cultures. This doesn't take anything away from a founder, a CEO or a leader. In fact, you avoid envy or jealousy by replacing it with respect and humility. We think that Walt Disney was right: "People hate big wheels and leaders who hog the show."

There are some leaders who just can't bring themselves to practice this concept because they must be the center of attention. Their lack of self-esteem prevents them from elevating any other person. We have observed that leaders who get in trouble over their credibility and ability to build a team often insist on being the number one hero in their own company.

We recommend that you consider a Borrowed Hero in building a culture that fosters a creative climate.

Dreama

The Hilton Inn West in Orlando served as the Disney training center during the construction and startup phase of Walt Disney World. Mike was having dinner there one evening with his sister Cynthia Titus when Roy and Edna Disney came in and took their seats at a table across the other side of the huge dining room. That evening, Roy Disney revealed the kind of behavior that establishes a creative climate.

There was a young waitress at the Hilton that night, a Disney employee by the name of Dreama. She was a high-spirited bubbly young woman who made a terrific waitress and a good Disney representative.

Dreama came up to Mike's table and asked, "Do you think Mr. Disney would mind if I went over and spoke to him? I admire him so much, but I've never seen him before. Would he be offended if I intruded upon his private dinner? I just want to tell him what a wonderful thing Disney World is for central Florida. There are jobs here now, plus excitement because we're all part of the Disney dream. What do you think?"

"Go ahead," Mike said. "Walk right over there, introduce yourself to Roy. If it makes you more comfortable, tell him Mike told you to do it. But express your feelings to him because I know he'll appreciate your gratitude."

She was still hesitant, but she eventually made her way over to Roy's table. Mike saw her speaking to him. Roy stood up, shook Dreama's hand and introduced her to his wife, Edna. Mike couldn't hear the conversation, although he certainly would have liked to!

About 10 minutes later, Roy got up from his table and walked over to Mike's table. Roy said, "Mike, I want to thank you for encouraging that girl, Dreama, to come over and introduce herself to me. What she said was very touching. I thank you for helping her to do it. After all, it's the Dreamas that make our Disney family work."

The wise man

E. Cardon Walker, Mike's boss (whose profile you read at the end of Chapter 1), once asked Mike to say a few words about Disney University and the Management Development Program at a conference being held at the studio for a group of theater owners. Mike told the story of the "Wise Man and the Little Boy" at this meeting, a story Walt heard from the back of the theater. He later repeated Mike's story for a 7-year-old boy at Disneyland.

The boy had spotted Walt in the park near Sleeping Beauty's Castle. His mother told him that Walt was one of the wisest and smartest men in the world. The boy approached Walt and said, "I understand that you are one of the wisest men in the world, Mr. Disney."

Walt said, "Well I don't know about that. Where are you folks from, anyway?"

The mother replied. "We're from Terre Haute, Indiana, Mr. Disney."

"Call me Walt. Well, young fellow, I'll tell you a story I heard the other day about a wise man. If you follow the advice in the story, you could grow up to become a wise man, too." And then he passed along the story he had heard from Mike.

"A little boy said to the wisest man in the world, 'How can I grow up to be a wise man like you?' The wise man said, 'There are four words that can guide you. Do these four things, and you will have the opportunity to become a wise man. Here are the four words.

" 'The first word, little boy, is *think*. Think about the values and principles that you believe in.

" 'The second word, little boy, is *believe*. Believe in yourself, based on the thinking you've done about your values and principles.

" 'The third word, little boy, is *dream*. Dream about something you want to do, based on your belief in yourself and based on the thinking you've done about your values and principles.

" 'The fourth word, little boy, is *dare*. Dare to make your dreams come true, based on your belief in yourself, based on the thinking you've done about your values and principles.' "

Walt placed his hand on the little boy's shoulder and said, "Just in case you forget these four words, let me repeat them: *think, believe, dream* and *dare*."

Those four words will help you break out of the box. Walt and Roy Disney practiced them in everything they did throughout their illustrious careers.

The Disney Brothers' Breakout Qualities

- ◆ Forming productive partnerships
- ◆ Using Imagineering
- ◆ Focusing on constant improvement
- ◆ Being technology-wise
- ◆ Using borrowed heroes
- ◆ Getting commitment

BREAKTHROUGH TECHNIQUES

ATMOSPHERES FOR ACHIEVEMENT

☑ Select a place where the team will work. Enrich it. Make it a Team Center or A Kitchen for the Mind. (See our book *Think Out of the Box* for more details on these dynamic environments.) It's best if the spot can be a permanent or semipermanent environment that is dedicated to work on the project for its duration. It may be part of the organization's existing architecture and corporate culture. Off-site facilities work, too!

☑ Equip the environment with creative resources along with necessary technology, furniture and materials. Gather tools for stimulating creative thought.

☑ Put someone in charge of the facility and environment. Secure the environment if necessary.

☑ Make sure the environment and *modus operandi* are creative, informative and participative. (We recommend the Creative Thinking Techniques System, described in our book *Think Out of the Box*.) Bottom line: Make sure you get input from others.

☑ Keep the ideas flowing. Capture all the ideas. Keep the environment organized and visually stimulating. Use Displayed Thinking.

☑ Have a good time. Loosen up! Are you having fun yet?

☑ Stimulate creative thinking: Use all your senses.

☑ Plan vicarious experiences.

☑ Establish special terminologies, symbols, rituals, and traditions.

☑ Celebrate victories along the way. Schedule parties and celebrations.

☑ Describe your corporate culture. How will you grow it?

CHAPTER 5

Motivating Yourself and Others

*"Ah, but a man's reach should exceed his grasp,
Or what's a heaven for?"*

—Robert Browning

Breaking out of the box means being self-motivated. People are self-motivated by what they consider to be important to them, which is based on their values.

We don't believe that there are any truly unmotivated people running around because one has to be motivated just to survive. Conflicts arise when individuals are motivated in a different direction than the one you believe they should be, either because of your own interests or those of your organization. The few people you may tend to think of as unmotivated are motivated, but in a less-than-constructive direction. Nearly everyone is motivated to achieve something.

People who have faced the challenge of bringing up children know well that kids are always motivated in some direction. The trick is channeling that motivation into an area that's likely to leave the house intact and the neighbors still talking to you at the end of the day.

The challenge is to create the desire for achievement within yourself first and within others later—if motivation is to be based on a solid foundation.

Ideally, you start where people are right now and proceed from there. The more you understand other people's needs, their rational self-interests—and your own, as well—the greater the possibility for establishing a self-motivating atmosphere. Instead of trying to fight rational self-interest, let it work in the organization's interest. Therefore, the question is: What does the person in question really need in order to feel appreciated for a particular field of expertise, or to feel safe, or to feel like part of the group, or to fulfill a personal challenge? Each of these needs represents a specific level of development.

Find the need! Then come up with a strategy for tying your project to that need, instead of imposing a superficial, rule book-oriented motivation theory to the task.

Too many goals are tied to factors that have nothing to do with the needs and values of the people who are supposedly being motivated. If people are intimidated into performing tasks, the tasks may get done, but breakthrough solutions will rarely result. When managing others, you must inspire them to accept tasks willingly, without browbeating them. If you haven't read Abraham Maslow's classic book *Motivation and the Human Personality*, you owe yourself the treat of experiencing this landmark achievement of behavioral psychology. Maslow's remains the seminal example when it comes to understanding human needs. Being sensitive to those needs produces the kind of mutual respect that causes one person to follow another up the hill. (By the way, you will also find the book extremely enlightening if your primary aim is to motivate yourself.)

What you hear, what you experience, what you expect

What you hear about yourself, especially what you hear at "the top of the stairs" during childhood, affects what you actually accomplish for the rest of your life. What you experience in childhood is of monumental importance in determining your own level of constructive self-motivation as well as the nature and intensity of the expectations you bring to your relationships with others.

Human expectations—the achievements people plan during their lifetimes— are what the breakthrough facilitate or must consider when enlisting human passion and energy to achieve a goal. This is a Herculean task, but one that must be undertaken.

We believe there are five major, overriding expectations that are present in everyone at some level. The inspired breakthrough facilitator will find ways to harness the attainment of goals to help fulfill each of these five expectations.

This is difficult since each of the five major expectations involves relationships with other people.

The following five expectations reflect what everyone wants out of life. The degree to which people are self-motivated to undertake a goal depends on the degree to which they believe the goal furthers one or more of these key expectations.

1. People expect that life will be just and that others will deal with them with integrity.

Even hardened cynics who bemoan the many cruelties of the world are acting on a basic assumption that life should be fair. Deep inside, everyone expects there to be some kind of fairness in the world.

One of the factors operating against people when they try to build relationships based on a presumption of fairness is the current nature of the mass media. People watch an excessive amount of television, listen to hours of radio and make a habit of reading newspapers and magazines. What are they learning from these sources? The mass media too often focus an inordinate amount of content on the tragic, the unjustifiable, the extreme, and discourage the notion that there are people who try to operate with a sense of fair play. Breakthrough facilitators must overcome these perceptions by using the force of their personalities and intellectual capacities. The finest breakthrough facilitator is one who exemplifies fairness and honesty.

These principles we're discussing may seem saccharine at first, but part of that has to do with the pervasive influence of the modern mass media. If we use these ideas and follow them as standards of conduct, we'll automatically overcome the prejudices that are part of living in the modern media age. We'll realize that the fairness we long for is really possible.

We conducted a study among our clients not long ago to find out what people actually looked for in a leader. We asked them to list the qualities and characteristics of an effective leader. We weren't surprised to learn that the number-one characteristic people looked for in a leader was fairness.

If people perceive waste, fraud and abuse all around them, they probably will not feel a sense of loyalty to their organization. People want to know that their work is being done for someone who isn't going to cut corners, engage in favoritism or nepotism or otherwise play games with their lives. They want to know they're being treated fairly. Then they're more likely to be motivated to focus their energies toward the organization's goals.

When you make a habit of treating people fairly and establish a reputation for fairness and integrity, you lay the foundations for a motivated, strongly cohesive work group. Morale problems become rare.

Integrity produces fairness because it adheres to a code of positive values. Breakthroughs will occur more often where there is integrity.

2. People expect authenticity.

Beware of the Chameleon Complex, named for the small lizard that changes its colors to match its surroundings. Chameleon "leadership" (which is no leadership at all) destroys authenticity.

If you adapt one set of values until you get what you want, and then adapt another set of values after you have what you want, you fall victim to the Chameleon Complex.

You probably can remember experiences with people who appeared to embrace your values, appeared to look at the world as you do, appeared to agree with you on major premises—and then reversed themselves by doing the opposite of what you'd been led to believe they would do. Such people were revealing a Chameleon Complex.

Everyone practices the Chameleon Complex at least occasionally. The question is, does it represent your preferred method of operation? Do you instinctively engage in chameleon techniques? Do you make a habit of showing one color when it suits you, then show a completely different color when you need to win over someone else? In private, you may have values that are very different from those you adapt temporarily. You become authentic when differences between doing one thing, saying another and believing still another no longer exist. Although it is not easy to eradicate completely, the Chameleon Complex should be acknowledged as a destructive human practice because it is essentially phony and because it leads to unrealistic thinking. It is worth trying to eliminate it wherever it appears.

The people who can become self-motivated breakthrough workers are normally mature enough to respect differences of opinion and style. Don't try to hide those differences by pretending to be someone you're not. Authentic behavior leads to respect.

The effective breakthrough facilitator doesn't send false images to people by putting up a front. Instead, the facilitator reflects values that remain consistent between interchanges. These are the values that others learn to expect, even though they may not always agree with the outcomes.

Of course, you have the potential to learn and change over time. But you want to leave people with the impression that you're charting a clear course, one they can believe in. If they discover that you only embrace their values while you're in the same room with them, the result will be disappointment and demotivation.

There are many situations where you have to use tact and diplomacy in what you say to people. But you can be sensitive to a situation and be authentic at the same time. People sense where your true values are.

It's important that people get the right message from you. If self-motivation is to be the result, the message has to be authentic. Motivation flourishes where there is an authentic response to needs, based on authentic values rather than the Chameleon Complex.

3. People expect that they will experience acceptance and understanding.

Mike had a memorable high school teacher by the name of Marge Graft. She taught American history. One of the requirements in her class was to memorize and recite the names of all the presidents of the U.S.

Mike decided not to bother doing this. Being a "big wheel" class officer and radio personality as host of a program called "Teen Talk" that aired on Sundays, he thought he could slide through without bothering to commit the names to memory. He mistakenly thought he could get away with skipping the requirement. Marge Graft wasn't the kind of teacher who would let a student slide, and she gave Mike an "incomplete," which is essentially a failing grade.

Mike felt terrible. He went to see Miss Graft at home one night on his way to a school dance. "I came to apologize," Mike said. "I should have memorized the names of the presidents, and I didn't. You were right, and I was wrong."

Miss Graft smiled and asked him to come in. She didn't offer to change the grade, but she and Mike became friends from that point on. Mike became a better student as a result of the attitude his teacher displayed. Even though Miss Graft had a firm set of standards that she was not willing to compromise, she was still able to impart a sense of belonging and acceptance to Mike and her other students. That's the mark of a great teacher.

Years later, as an adult, Mike was invited to give a speech at his high school in which he paid tribute to his old history teacher, the woman who had taught him such respect for learning. He told the story of how he became a better student as the result of a teacher who gave him an "incomplete," then invited him into her home. Mike's speech stressed that his performance—not meeting his obligation to memorize and recite the names of the presidents—had caused the incomplete in history. At the end of the speech, he recited the names of all the presidents of the U.S., and thanked Miss Graft, who was seated in the front row of the auditorium, for her gift of teaching and for her acceptance of him as a person. She had taught Mike a valuable lesson.

After the speech, Mike was summoned to the principal's office. Imagine, a grown man being summoned to the principal's office! Waiting for him there were both the principal and Miss Graft, who had opened up his transcript. As Mike watched, she wrote "completed" next to the line for the history course.

She said, "Mike, you've improved a lot since high school, but you still have a long way to go. But people should get credit for everything they deserve to get credit for." Then she smiled that warm smile of hers.

Accepting and understanding the people you work with is not the same as exempting them from standards. It is, instead, a necessary prerequisite for helping them achieve the goals associated with those standards.

You must balance your use of standards with an appreciation and acceptance of people as individuals. You must understand their need for fulfillment and acceptance at the same time that you expect great performances from them, and you must never withhold that understanding in the hope of intimidating them into achieving for you.

4. People expect to deal with rational human beings.

Two headlines we came across recently caught our attention. They read:

Gun sales are up to protect us from the nuts

Gated communities boom to protect us from doom

What a sorry "community" these headlines represent! What do they tell society about its perceptions of life? They could discourage even the most positive thinker.

In spite of such messages, there are people you can count on, and the breakthrough facilitator has to be one of those people. This person has to be honest, capable of seeing issues clearly and calmly and willing to invest the time and energy necessary for the development of long-term relationships.

When organizations talk about partnerships, *esprit de corps* and rapport among team members, what they're really talking about is the art of building friendship.

The best breakthrough facilitators understand the fine art of building friendships. The best breakthrough facilitators build not opportunistic relationships but friendships with the people with whom they work, and they accomplish this because they are rational and trustworthy individuals who aren't out to score points in the short term or manipulate others for personal advantage. We think a valid definition of the word "friend" incorporates this idea of rationality.

A friend is someone who takes a rational approach, rather than an adversarial approach, to a long-term relationship. And it's the ability to count on rational people over the long term that builds strong breakthrough organizations. Adversarial relationships, on the other hand, tend to create conflict and enemies. That process puts people in the box.

People who get boxed in often engage in unproductive bluffing, bullying and begging, whereas out-of-the-box thinkers are realistic, democratic and productive.

5. People expect that life will be exciting.

Who actually sets out for work in the morning hoping it will be dull?

Nobody! In fact, most people start out feeling at least a little refreshment, a little charge at the beginning of the day. The prospect of a new day can be an exciting one.

And yet, somehow, business is often dull and unfulfilling. The quest for excitement and stimulation is among the most powerful human expectations—and yet this desire is typically ignored in setting up organizations, goals, plans and strategies. People revert to relying on the predictable, the proven, the familiar, the routine, and leave out the excitement of newness in work.

Even children can't escape parents who try to manage the "fun" in their lives. The result? No excitement! It's the same for team members. One of the best practices you can adopt in working with people is to outline a challenge for them and then stand back and let them go. You need to find a way to say "Go for it!" a thousand times a day!

Rather than controlling the individuals you're working with, present them with an example of what to do, then be willing to let them achieve. Issuing too many instructions can be restrictive, numbing and boring. Setting a loose set of guidelines—and then encouraging individuals to take advantage of new opportunities within those guidelines—is exciting. It's important to recognize, of course, that there are some activities that require training with absolute standards and adherence to specific instructions. In these situations, other motivational techniques need to be used. In most cases, however, there is little or nothing to lose, and everything to gain, by helping people to get a charge out of what they do and by maintaining areas in which they are free to experiment.

Let people discover what the new trends are in their area of expertise. Let them develop a working knowledge of the latest technologies that affect what they do. Let your people take time to build a knowledge base before they attempt to achieve a particular task. Let them experiment with new ways of working within a loosely structured model. (These days, people call that model the "boundaryless culture.") In a supportive way, monitor the experiments; help the team focus on what works and discard what doesn't.

Let people find out something new about what they do, features they haven't experienced before. Let them participate in the organization's accumulation of new data, and give them credit for what they discover. This will bring excitement into the office.

We developed a formula for remembering the most important factors to keep track of while finding the best ways to incorporate this sense of newness into people's work:

T-N-T (Technology-Needs-Trends)

What new technologies are being used to accomplish what you're trying to accomplish? What's going on in research? What's being launched? What's appropriate for your organization one, two or five years down the line? How are you tied into and informed about developing trends? What are your sources?

What needs do these technologies fulfill? Who is the intended market? What needs does your organization have right now?

What trends have emerged from the union of a particular technology with a particular need? How have the technologies in question changed what people do? How are the technologies in question likely to change what people do? How will they affect you?

The Creative Thinking Association of America publishes a monthly audio-cassette magazine called *The Brain Exchange* that is designed to help you track new developments in Technologies-Needs-Trends. It can be very helpful as you try to search for new ways to inspire and motivate people to find a sense of challenge and excitement in the work they do for your organization.

The right "streetcar"

Encouraging self-motivation means meeting human expectations. As the famed playwright Tennessee Williams might have put it, the key is to get people onto that "streetcar named desire"—their desire—and headed in a purposeful direction, rather than working aimlessly or unproductively.

Ideally, you should pursue a path that exposes you to people who are just and honest, accepting, understanding, rational and exciting. At the same time, self-motivation means being true to yourself. It means finding ways not to head in a direction that is in conflict with your own values. It means rejecting those practices and activities that you know will demotivate you.

When Mike was a little boy, his grandfather ran a grocery store in Greenville, Ohio. Mike wanted a new fly rod so he could go fishing at nearby Wayne Lakes. He asked his grandfather if he could have one as a present. His grandfather said no, but offered to let him earn the fly rod by working at the grocery store. So it was that Mike was sent down into the basement of the store to sort the potatoes.

There in the basement Mike discovered that he had companions: rats. Big ones, and plenty of them. Mike clearly remembers his decision to find a way not to expose himself to a life that featured work alongside these four-legged "partners" as part of his later life. Those rats put him on the "streetcar named desire"—fast! That's self-motivation.

What motivated Diane as a little girl was a desire to have the toy that everyone else in the neighborhood had: a yo-yo. But she had to work for it. So her father made a deal with her: For every dandelion she pulled in the yard, she'd receive a penny. Yo-yos were going for a dollar apiece at the time. Diane diligently removed exactly 100 dandelions. Diane got her dollar and went to the corner store, hoping to buy her brand-new yo-yo...which is when she learned, as we all must, about the concept of taxes. She didn't have enough to buy the yo-yo after all! So she had to go back home and dig a few more dandelions to get the extra pennies for the taxman. She did it, and she got her yo-yo. She was also on the "streetcar named desire" with another strong objective: to find a more rewarding and lucrative occupation than dandelion-picking!

Rats and dandelions planted the seeds for self-motivation for us. They sparked needs and actions that eventually led to achievement and fulfillment.

What's the first thing that got you on that streetcar?

Summary

➢ People are self-motivated by what they consider to be important to them. The "streetcar named desire" is made up of their deep-seated values.

➢ Constructive self-motivation must arise out of strong, preexisting needs. Fighting those needs is pointless. The objective is to point them in the right direction.

➢ There are five major expectations that must be considered when dealing with issues of self-motivation.

1. People expect that life will be just and that others will deal with them fairly.

2. People expect authenticity. (Chameleon Complex "leadership"—which is no leadership at all—destroys authenticity.)

3. People expect that they will experience acceptance and understanding.

4. People expect to deal with rational human beings.

5. People expect that life will be exciting.

Profile: Self-motivation

Val J. Halamandaris

*National Association for HomeCare, The Caring Institute,
Founder and CEO; Author*

Self-motivation is a personality attribute considerably more precious than gold. It moves mountains, helps create solutions and brings hope out of despair.

People who possess self-motivation bring into existence most of the world's products and solve most of the world's problems. They act rather than talk. They are the dreamers, the doers, the movers and shakers.

Our close friend, Val J. Halamandaris, is one of these people. He always seems to find a way to do something about the things that need doing. He is a fantastic contributor, eager to make life better for thousands of people. He champions an endless list of causes, especially care for the aged.

Val's career traces the rise of a young boy working in the coal mines, a boy who eventually became an influential lawyer on Capitol Hill, a counsel to U.S. Senators, an adviser to Presidents, an author, a publisher and an entrepreneur. His is a very special, very American story that is truly inspiring.

From coal mines to the halls of government

Val started out life in a coal mining community, and later became counsel to Congressman Claude Pepper's House Select Committee on Aging. For 15 years, Val was counsel to Senator Frank E. Moss of Utah (who is now retired) and the U.S. Senate Special Committee on Aging. Val is widely recognized as an expert on health care and aging.

Val J. Halamandaris received wide recognition and respect for his courageous investigations exposing abuse and fraud against the elderly. The insight he gained motivated him to address this challenging issue in health care. He has authored numerous books on the subject, and he is editor and publisher of two national magazines, *Caring* and *Caring People*—publications that present scholarly papers on health care problems, profiles of outstanding health caregivers and information about new treatment developments and protocols.

He helped found the "National Caring Awards," a recognition program by which the Caring Institute recognizes caring men and women in America. He is also president of the National Association for HomeCare (NAHC), a position he has occupied since the group was founded in 1982. Under his inspirational leadership, NAHC has achieved significant growth, unparalleled legislative success and is regarded as one of the most progressive associations in Washington, D.C.

Val is the founder and the driving force behind the creation of two Washington, D.C., Museums: The Hall of Fame for Caring Americans and the Hall of Honor for Congress. Congressman Claude Pepper, in a tribute placed in the Congressional Record, said, "Val J. Halamandaris has demonstrated a deep and lasting commitment to the betterment of our country. He has done much to restore confidence in our government and to earn the respect of the Congress and the people of the United States."

Val's HomeCare Association brings thousands of caregivers together into a dynamic organization that provides them with valuable resources and tools to be even better in their important work. He helps them build self-esteem, which leads to self-motivation.

Val and his dedicated brother, Bill Halamandaris, are philanthropic entrepreneurs whose contributions in fighting for the proper treatment of the elderly are legendary. Dr. Arthur S. Flemming, former Secretary of Health, Education and Welfare, told us, "Val is one of the greatest advocates for seniors in America. He goes beyond the call of duty every time."

Margaret (Peg) Cushman, president of the Visiting Nurses Association, told us that without Val the cause for aging Americans would be back in the dark ages. She said, "He has brought the problems, the challenges and the opportunities out in the open for everyone to look at. He is a visionary pointing the direction for us." Undoubtedly, our national awareness of the problem of aging and related health care issues has been heightened and furthered by Val's tireless work.

Senator Frank E. Moss said of Val, "Although he has chosen to stay in the background, he deserves much of the credit for what was accomplished both at the U.S. Senate Special Committee on Aging, where he was closely associated with me, and at the House Select Committee on Aging, where he was Congressman Claude Pepper's senior counsel and closest advisor. He put together more hearings on the subject of aging, wrote more reports, drafted more bills and had more influence on the direction of events than anyone before him or since. After five years of research, Val took six months in 1994 to produce what many people believe was the best and most impressive series of congressional reports ever written on the subject of aging and health care for seniors. He wrote a 12-volume series titled *Nursing Home Care in the United*

States. The report was a scorching indictment of America's nursing home industry. The research and the mountain of data were so compelling that no one could quarrel with its conclusions, the primary one being that 50 percent of the nursing homes in the Unites States were substandard with one or more life-threatening conditions."

We first met Senator Moss when he attended a Creative Thinking Seminar conducted by Mike in Boston. We had a memorable dinner with him and the board members of the National Association for HomeCare. He helped us to understand how extraordinary our friend Val was and the magnitude of his devotion to great causes. His achievements would easily fill a book.

He also gave us insight into the role of Val's brother, Bill Halamandaris, as the two battled Medicare and Medicaid fraud in their crusade against corrupt practices. As Senator Moss put it, "The crucial role of Bill Halamandaris should also be mentioned. Val reached out to his brother when he needed help. We were knee-deep in our pursuit of organized crime and its involvement in Medicare and Medicaid. Val needed someone he could trust and turned to Bill. The year that the Halamandaris brothers worked together on the staff of the U.S. Senate Committee on Aging marks the high point in the committee's history. Bill was the perfect complement to Val. Quietly efficient and with a great eye for detail, he more and more took on the job of chief investigator and field general."

The Halamandaris brothers' unrelenting crusade included investigating the "dumping" of patients by state mental hospitals into boarding homes, Medicaid Mills with phony bills, swindlers' schemes against the elderly and the HUD scandal. It is said "for every dragon that is born, a Saint George is born to slay it." The Halamandaris brothers are dragon slayers.

The spirit of self-motivation

In a recent discussion, Diane described Val's spirit of self-motivation in this way:

"I received a telephone call in my office back in 1983 from a man requesting Mike Vance to speak to his organization at an upcoming meeting. The man's voice on the phone was extremely kind and sincere, qualities that I don't encounter often enough. From the beginning of our conversation, I could sense that the goals and objectives of his organization were not going to be the normal hard-hitting, bottom-line, number-crunching, cut-to-the-chase stuff. We began to discuss his newly formed organization. I knew behind this kind, intelligent voice was the beginning of a unique organization that really cared about what they were doing and how they were doing it.

"I then discovered that what they truly cared about was people. He said the organization's name was the National Association for HomeCare. They were at the beginning of what would turn out to be exploding growth and expansion bringing together home care, hospice care and visiting nurses groups.

"The man's name was Val J. Halamandaris. Little did I know that some years later, Val would be a close personal friend of mine and introduce me in Washington to the President of the United States!

"We discussed the content of Mike's speech for the presentation to Val's group. It became obvious to me that he would select one of Mike's deep intellectual topics, Management by Values. The focus of this series is developing your values into a culture that unites values, standards and goals together. The emphasis is on using top-line thinking to produce high performance bottom-line results.

"We discovered in working with Val that he had the key ingredient necessary to grow and develop anything: self-motivation. He had an internal, self-motivating drive. He was going to help the American health care system break out of the box by going beyond traditional roles and into creative new approaches.

"Since then, we have continued to develop a very special friendship. I have looked to Val as a role model and mentor in my personal growth. He has been generous and inspiring to me in so many ways, including his giving a copy of our book *Think Out of the Box* to the President of the United States!

"I once asked Val how he stayed so motivated. He said, 'The more you give to others, the more you get back, which recharges the spirit and motivates you to continue on.' Later, I told Mike that a kind of spiritual glue holds Val together for the purpose of 'slaying dragons' and giving birth to new, caring, people-oriented organizations."

"Mother values"

Mike once shared a memorable private dinner with Val. As Mike recalls it, "We had an intimate dinner that has stood out in my memory among a large number of dinner meetings that I have in my kind of work. I remember it well because I was a little disturbed about something, and Val lifted my spirits by really listening to me and by being sincerely concerned with what was on my mind that night. He encouraged me with practical suggestions aimed right at my need. His approach caused me not to merely brush off the issue, but to examine it.

"He told me to draw on my inner strength and reservoir of values. He told me to think of 'mother values,' which I had never heard of in this context. Val defined 'mother values' as the answers to questions our mothers challenged us to ask ourselves. Sometimes, these answers are set—and reinforced over the years—without a word ever being spoken. He said these values are 'the fountainhead of self-motivation.' "

As it happened, Val's mother had died recently, and Mike's wasn't too well. "Mother values," Mike learned, lie at the heart of everyone's motivation. These values, for better or worse, dwell in us forever, long after our mothers have graduated to the next dimension. At this dinner, Val taught Mike to look at himself carefully and to look carefully at others to see those "mother values" in their character and behavior. His advice: "Keep your mother's best values alive in your day-to-day living because it's the finest tribute you can pay to her memory."

Together, the two men explored just what some of those values might be. Great mothers have a way of keeping their children focused on searching for the big issues in life. They stimulate them to probe the cosmological questions. Later, Val listed these imponderable questions in his magnificent book, *Faces of Caring: A Search for the 100 Most Caring People in History*. They are universal questions, important to all who seek answers on their journey through life. They will stimulate your philosophical thinking, just as they have done for us.

Cosmological Questions/Mother Values

Why are we born?	What is greatness?
Why do we live?	What is wealth?
Why do we suffer?	What is service?
What is the meaning of life?	What is freedom?
What is love?	What is a hero?
What is truth?	What are good and evil?
What is justice?	What is selfishness?
What is integrity?	What is caring?
What is courage?	What is the secret of graceful aging?
What is excellence?	Why do we die?
What is success?	What is the proper measure of
What is happiness?	human life?

These questions could be a syllabus for a course on life. These eternal questions challenge finite human beings to probe deeper, go further and get under the surface of things. That's the kind of person Val is—a pathfinder to discovering truth.

Mike recalled a saying Val had: "Life is like a big jigsaw puzzle with tremendous gain available to humanity as the pieces are assembled." This idea helped Mike put the content together for a meeting with the HomeCare executives. Because the entire health care industry is at a point where the pieces need to be assembled for the synergy they can create, the people at this meeting could help achieve this synergy.

Understanding history at a deep level

Val once asked his grandmother why the Greeks had tumbled from their lofty heights. "Because they became selfish and fought among themselves," she answered.

Val's understanding of history goes deep and brings depth to his works. "Human beings alone," he once observed, "have the ability to transfer learning from one generation to another. We now have the benefits of thousands of years of recorded history." This insight underscores how sacred every single life is, how everyone can succeed by asking the right questions and how learning from past experiences, and from each other, should be a primary occupation.

We are happy to know a man like Val, who has served as both mentor and friend to Diane, and as both student and teacher to Mike. He exemplifies those superlative, energized values that make for a self-motivated human being.

Val J. Halamandaris's Breakout Qualities

- ◆ Caring outlook
- ◆ Sensitivity
- ◆ Self-motivation
- ◆ Creative approach
- ◆ Commitment
- ◆ Devotion to scholarship
- ◆ Loving attitude

BREAKTHROUGH TECHNIQUES

MAXIMUM UTILIZATION OF TALENT

☑ Are the team members you select self-motivated people? Do you have a motivational and/or inspirational team leader? Try to get motivated people who are grounded and reality-based.

☑ Find the need levels, self-interests and background of the team members to get them charged!

☑ If there is limited motivation among the team, bring in some motivational resources. (Not the superficial type—but the deep philosophical stuff. Of course, we recommend our Creative Thinking Association team!)

☑ Select a professional facilitator for the creative thinking sessions. The facilitator must get the team's motivation channeled in the right direction for breakthroughs to occur. How will this be done?

☑ Build team friendships for long-term relationships.

☑ Identify trends, needs and technology as they relate to your project.

☑ Breakthroughs require high energy. Is the team energized?

☑ Establish the team rewards for accomplishing breakthroughs.

☑ Ask yourself what tools, techniques and resources should be used to motivate yourself and others.

CHAPTER 6

Pursuing Mastery

*"Order and simplification are the first steps toward
the mastery of a subject..."*

—Thomas Mann

The master archer aimed his bow and arrow intently toward the distant target, one that was barely visible in the morning fog. His breathing seemed suspended. His chest was still. He waited in silence for the right moment, and then he let the arrow fly off the bowstring, cutting through to the exact center of the target. Bull's-eye!

Mastery is the attainment of unequaled skill and knowledge. It leads to breakthroughs and superiority in whatever endeavor is undertaken. Mastery is proficiency of the highest rank. Masters display exceptional ability, expertise, command and know-how. They boast matchless skills.

Do you remember the stages of ability we discussed earlier in the book? They were: ignorance, awareness, knowledge and wisdom. Mastery begins to emerge as we attain wisdom.

Many people make the mistake of confusing mastery—a long-term outlook on life—and success, which is usually tied to a particular outcome and contrasted with failure. Mastery is a process, and there is a considerable difference between success and mastery!

A growing phenomenon toward seeking mastery is taking place in the business world today. One CEO we know expressed his conviction that "we want to be better than the best." He meant that he didn't consider "the best" to be good enough! That's a mastery-oriented outlook.

We've worked with people around the world, and we've noticed that the trend in breakthrough leadership is going even beyond excellence and culminating in mastery. We believe that this is part of a general trend toward greater value and meaning in our relationships at all levels.

Mastery of the 5 equities*

There are five basic equities that prepare us to become masters in a chosen field or activity: physical equity, intellectual equity, spiritual equity, psychological equity and financial equity. Each of the five equities needs to be in balance in our lives if we are to become masters. Each establishes a holistic area of harmony in our lives. Each helps us break out of the box.

The development of all five equities produces the highest rank of mastery: the grand master. Those who attain this ultimate rank change the world by their insights and their personal examples. They *break out of the box.*

We hope you will be aroused, stimulated, *motivated* to join us in the quest for mastery. As Miss Mae Carden, whose profile you read in Chapter 2, said, "Don't be ordinary. Don't be average. We already have enough of ordinary and average." We hope you'll catch this spirit when you read the profile at the end of this chapter of a notable grand master of our day, Mr. Jack Nicklaus.

Physical equity

Physical equity has to do with maintaining the body in the best possible condition throughout the changing seasons of life. Masters run their bodies; their bodies don't run them.

Prolonged overindulgence in tacos, hot fudge sundaes and margaritas—as necessary as these items may be for *occasional* breakthroughs—make physical equity a high hurdle for most of us. The master can control the body's appetites in many ways, most of them rooted in training and a hard-won discipline.

Practitioners of yoga or the physical disciplines of the far eastern religions set marvelous examples in the area of physical equity. (The film *The Karate Kid* inspired younger people to reach for higher levels of physical mastery.)

It's difficult to become a master without pursuing physical equity. Some authorities would argue that it's impossible!

---

* The word "equity" is being used here to mean that which increases in value with age.

Intellectual equity

A master is committed to learning as a permanent part of life. Masters play on a stage in which the pursuit of knowledge is a constant drive. They know that the more they learn, the more there will be to learn. As a result, masters never engage in posturing when it comes to "knowing more" than someone else. They don't brag about their knowledge or flaunt their intellectual superiority. (See Chapter 1 for a discussion of the stages of ability.)

Spiritual equity

Spiritual equity has to do with the belief that we are part of a meaningful, purposeful universe, a universe that has behind it a design and certain general principles. When masters embrace spiritual equity, they acknowledge that life has a purpose, that it is valuable. Masters know that we are not meant to be passengers on a rudderless ship that drifts along aimlessly. There is a reason for the journey we have undertaken in this life.

Spiritual equity gives us a sense of connectivity in life. Masters know that we are part of the universe, not aliens within it.

Spirituality can be present in each of the four acknowledged theological positions. They are: atheism, in which one denies the existence of God, but can believe that there is organization demonstrated in the universe; theism, in which one believes in the existence of God; deism, in which one believes that the existence of God is demonstrated by nature but rejects formal religion; and agnosticism, in which one holds that the existence of God cannot be logically proved or disproved. None of these positions precludes the development of spirituality as we've defined it.

Masters of spirituality tend to be caring, charitable and concerned; they are often activists for moral causes. They inspire people and show them how to turn principles into reality.

Psychological equity

Psychological equity means liking and accepting oneself. It means being comfortable with what you are and maintaining a healthy sense of self-esteem.

Mastery in this equity is challenging, because it means moving beyond feelings of guilt. This is different from denying guilt. One must *understand* guilt. Those with strong psychological equity understand their actions and the feelings that arise from them, rather than trying to evade or deny those feelings.

Self-acceptance is a hallmark of those who possess psychological equity. While no one is "free" of guilt, as you approach mastery, you can see events in perspective, adjust your ways of dealing with people and learn to be free from the effects of guilt. In this way, you can keep guilt from harming you and instead use it as a positive force for change.

Financial equity

At the most elementary level, financial equity means having enough money to meet the needs for subsistence. Beyond this interpretation, people must decide how much money they need to fulfill their desires. What is enough? That depends on the situation.

To most people, it would appear that Bill Gates and Warren Buffett have "enough" money. But this can't be judged without knowing what they're trying to accomplish!

Financial equity is essential to survival, but it is frequently overemphasized. People often treat money as if it were the only measure of status and achievement, although it is a grave mistake to make this assumption.

By overemphasizing the need for money, one runs the risk of neglecting development in the other four areas. The Buddha emphasized what is known as "right livelihood," the most harmonious means of attaining one's living. A true master develops an attitude about financial equity that keeps everything within a framework of proper personal development. Masters have a healthy perspective about money: It doesn't control them; they control it.

The 5 major areas of philosophy

In addition to the five equities, there are five major areas in philosophy that, when understood, lead to the attainment of mastery, which in turn can lead to breakthroughs. These five categories are: metaphysics, epistemology, ethics, politics and aesthetics. (Refer to page 126 for examples of issues explored within each category.)

Metaphysics

Metaphysics is the study of the root causes of things. It has to do with the essential nature of life's events. Metaphysics offers an overview of human existence. It is the main branch of philosophy.

There are two main personal metaphysical points of view. They can be summed up as follows: "Life is benevolent" and "Life is malevolent." The masters in metaphysics, of course, have come to that rich point in their lives where they see all of the yin and the yang and the plus and the minus—and understand, as Mother Teresa put it, "the shadows as well as the lights."

The essential metaphysical question to ask is, "How do I view life?"

Epistemology

The second branch of philosophy, epistemology, is the study of the nature and limits of knowledge. Masters focus on epistemology more than anybody. They ask: "How do you acquire knowledge?" It's such a basic question, and yet few people examine it.

Some of the great learners of the world, such as Confucius and Plato, pose and dedicate themselves to addressing questions of epistemology. They explore their personal experiences in life to see how those experiences led to meta-physical conclusions.

The essential epistemological question to ask is, "What have been my critical experiences in life?"

Ethics

Ethical philosophy has to do with a set of moral principles. It relates to the study of good and evil, and of moral duty.

Ethics represent the third area of philosophy. Ethics are the principles people use to govern their lives, to guide key decisions and to strengthen their goals. Ethics should guide you instinctively and help you feel certain about your path and your sense of what is right and wrong. Occasionally, of course, "gray areas" are encountered and that's when mastery in ethical issues takes on a reflective, self-examining character.

The essential ethical question to ask is, "What are the moral values I believe in as guiding principles?"

Politics

The fourth realm of philosophy is the study and practice of government and public affairs.

Epistemology

Metaphysical Junction

Constructive	Destructive
1. Life is benevolent	1. Life is malevolent
2. Cognitive reasoning	2. Unexplained injunction
3. Understanding	3. Confusion
4. Confidence	4. Uncertainty
5. Knowledge	5. Ignorance
6. Open	6. Closed
7. Up	7. Down
8. Wet	8. Dry
9. Friendly	9. Hostile
10. Hope	10. Despair
11. Growing	11. Dying
12. Still dreaming	12. Talk about others
13. Courageous	13. Fearful
14. Optimistic	14. Pessimistic

Ethical Structure

1. Justice	1. Ends justify means
2. Forthrightness	2. Chameleon Complex
3. Cooperation	3. Exploitation
4. Freely give credit	4. Plagiarize
5. Loving	5. Hateful
6. Forgiving, not excusing	6. Holding a grudge
7. Kindness	7. Abrasiveness
8. Share	8. Take
9. Original	9. Copying other people

Political

1. Good	1. Evil
2. Mutual respect	2. Suppression of values
3. Self-governing	3. Governed by others
4. Elected	4. Took over
5. Focus on the individual	5. Focus on society

Aesthetics

1. Appreciate beauty	1. Focus on ugly
2. Wide variety of tastes	2. Limited tastes
3. Fresh, naive	3. Routine
4. Sensory	4. Flat, inhibited

The focus here is not on being either Democrats or Republicans, but on how you feel about authoritarian, dictatorial governing of people as compared to a free and open society. Which of these two political models do you really embrace in your daily life?

It's not enough to *say* that you pursue a nonauthoritarian approach in your interactions with others. They (and you) can only benefit from an open approach if this approach is *actually implemented*.

The essential political question to ask is, "Do I believe people should be free, or should they be controlled?"

Aesthetics

The fifth area of philosophy deals with the study of beauty—in areas such as art, architecture, literature—and with the study of beauty itself. The dictionary defines aesthetics as "the branch of philosophy that is concerned with the nature of art and the criteria of artistic judgment." That definition may *sound* as though it's far removed from day-to-day, bottom-line concerns, but it isn't. Aesthetics is really the branch of philosophy that has to do with knowing what is good taste and what is not.

Aesthetic mastery helps you know that you are in tune with good design principles and with how to arrange things in the proper scale with one another. This is an extremely important part of facilitating breakthroughs.

The essential aesthetic question to ask is, "What do I consider beautiful?"

10 areas for mastery

These, then, are 10 areas for growth toward personal mastery. We feel they are an essential part of the effort to achieve breakthrough thinking. You can keep a list, a personal inventory, that will help you keep track of where you are in these 10 areas. Then use the ongoing results to design your personal Master's Program.

The Master's Program is what you believe you need to do in your work toward mastery in each one of these areas. After you find out where you are now, you can determine what steps to take to improve yourself in each area.

Your master's program: the 5 equities

Instructions: In the middle column, write a brief sentence describing your current assessment of yourself in the area in question. (For example, for physical equity you might write: "Generally good physical condition, low blood pressure, not overweight.") In the right hand column, fill in the steps you can take to help yourself grow in this area. (For example, "Continue exercise program, increase aerobic exercises to increase endurance.")

Equity	Where I am now	Steps I plan to take to grow in this area
Physical equity (Evaluate your physical condition and your general health.)		
Intellectual equity (Appraise those areas where your knowledge and intellect are challenged to expand.)		
Spiritual equity (Assess your attitudes toward life and your spiritual goals.)		
Psychological equity (Describe your current level of self-esteem and self-confidence.)		
Financial equity (What is your financial outlook?)		

Your master's program: the 5 areas of philosophy

Area	Where I am now	Steps I plan to take to grow in this area
Metaphysics (Do you regard life as generally benevolent or malevolent?)		
Epistemology (Have you come to terms with life experiences that have molded your character?)		
Ethics (How do you define the values that are most important to you?)		
Politics (Is your style of interaction with others essentially freedom-based or control-based?)		
Aesthetics (How do you incorporate beauty in your daily life?)		

We think these 10 areas apply to all aspects of life, not just to a single area.

The master appears in unexpected places

Mike had an unusual experience some years back that demonstrated how some masters appear in the places you'd least expect to see them. It occurred on a beautiful winter morning in Ohio after the snow had been falling all night. It was still coming down as the sun rose.

The trees were bare, revealing their magnificent structure against the pearl gray of the morning. Mike was sitting in his kitchen, eating some peanut butter toast and looking out the second-story window to a pathway leading to a barn, where he saw his friend Leo. Leo was shoveling snow off the walkways to the houses. It was a remarkable process: He would complete a long stretch of the walkway, stand back to examine his work, find two or three spots that he'd missed and then go back over the entire area. He did this over and over.

Mike ate several pieces of peanut butter toast as he watched Leo's routine continue. Mike found himself amazed at the excellence his friend brought to the task of removing snow. It seemed like such a menial task, especially for a man like Leo, who, as Mike knew, could do anything, build anything. Leo had no idea anyone was looking at him. He shoveled snow better than anyone Mike had ever seen. Maybe, Mike thought, Leo was a master snow-shoveler. Even the simple tasks, Mike realized, could be worthy objects of mastery.

You may remember the television miniseries *Shogun.* There was a scene in which a master archer, blindfolded, picked up a bow and fired an arrow. The arrow went right through a wall—and stuck to a pole set behind it. Then the archer, still blindfolded, picked up *another* arrow, fired it through the same hole, and split the first arrow! That's the master archer we described at the opening of this chapter.

What are some of the characteristics of masters? Leo exhibited one of them: Masters do something again and again until they get it right. Also, they don't care how humble a task appears. A very menial task doesn't result in any loss of care from a master; it still gets done with care and attention.

Another major characteristic of the master is the willingness *not to worry about the target.* Masters don't worry about their goals and objectives, because they always know they're going to *reach* them. They simply focus on doing whatever is required to reach the goal.

Masters *know* they've got all the tools—a magnificent bow, a perfect arrow, a set of fingers that form a perfect line when extended toward the middle of the palm—and they use the marvelous tools at their disposal in complete faith and understanding. Did you ever wonder just *how* our four fingers, all of different lengths, evolved to be able to form a straight line at the tips when curved down into the palm? We show this to children sometimes, and they spend considerable time moving their fingers back and forth, watching the line fall into place. They're taking steps toward understanding the principles of mastery!

One can do fairly well by setting goals and objectives, until faced by an opponent who's working under the philosophy of mastery. The master picks up the bow, loads the arrow, lets it *fall* off the bow at the perfect moment when everything is just right—and splits the other arrow.

There's a book you may enjoy called *Zen in the Art of Archery* by Eugen Herrigel. You can find it in the inspirational section of any well-stocked bookstore. It deals with the concept of mastery, too. It outlines a marvelous activity you can do with a child, an activity that sheds light on the idea of mastery.

Take a child outside on a snowy day. Sit under a tree that still has leaves. What happens? A leaf will pile up with snow until it can't hold any more, then it reaches what is referred to as "critical mass," and then the snow slips off, falls to the ground and the leaf pops back up. Watch as the leaf begins to accumulate snow again, so that it can repeat the entire process.

The source of mastery lies in allowing critical mass to be reached. That's the same ability the master archer used when he split the arrow. That was the point at which the arrow flew at the target.

A master knows when the time is right! Whether the subject is marketing, internal organization, product design or whatever—when everything is right, the correct action just flies off the bow and flies toward the heart of your target. Talk about a breakthrough! But one needs a superb sense of timing to pull it off and to practice continually in order to let the timing work.

Think of the legendary golfer Jack Nicklaus. There's a right time for him to assume his grip, and he holds that grip until the precise fraction of a second when everything is ready. Only when that point of critical mass appears does he address the ball. (Diane is still trying to master this one.)

Masters are *patient*. They know how to wait. They wait for critical mass. (That's called timing!) Masters know when the last piece of snow is falling on the top of the leaf, so that the leaf will slip down, empty itself and spring back up again.

Total devotion to the task at hand

Another example of a master at work involves a story about Mike's son Johnny and Steve Jobs, cofounder of Apple Computer, fishing for trout. They not only caught a tremendous amount of fish, but one fish, caught by Johnny, turned out to be a two-and-a-half pound trout. That's a big one. Johnny had it frozen, although Mike didn't know this. When it came time to return to Los Angeles, Mike found among Johnny's things the huge frozen fish wrapped in a hotel towel. (They had a talk about that appropriation of the towel later on.)

Mike knew there was no way he was going to get that fish away from his son. He wanted to take it back home and show it to his mother. So they decided to bring it on the plane.

By the time the trout got to Los Angeles, it was no longer a frozen trout; it was a drippy trout. As Johnny made his way up the driveway, he shouted to his mother, "Mom! I caught the biggest trout! Bigger than Steve Jobs's trout!"

His mother picked him up, drippy trout and all, and gave him a big hug. That's what a master breakthrough artist has to do sometimes: grab people who are holding drippy trouts.

Here was Johnny, almost 6 years old, and he was, according to the trout pro we spoke to later, already a master fisherman. When he went fishing, Johnny exhibited all the characteristics of the master. He wasn't worried about catching the fish, because he knew he was going to do what was required to catch one. He would *wait* until critical mass occurred.

Mastery in your field means full attention to detail

We once saw the concept of mastery demonstrated in a profound way by a bus driver. We were at Walt Disney World conducting a seminar and were riding the bus to go out to dinner with the president of a company attending our seminar. The driver, whose name was Hank, asked the president, "How are things going?"

The president said, "Really good!"

"Are you enjoying the park?" Hank asked.

"Oh, yes," replied the president.

"How are your accommodations?" Hank asked.

"Well, they're very nice," the president answered, "but I do have one problem. The hot water in my villa isn't hot enough."

"It's not?" Hank asked. "What villa are you in?"

"Villa 10," the president said.

While the bus pulled into a stop to pick up some more people, Hank got on the radio and said, "Maintenance? Joe, is that you? I've got a man here from Villa 10, and he's on his way to the Contemporary Hotel for dinner—very nice man. He's been having trouble getting hot water. And I wonder if, while he's having dinner at the hotel, you could get his hot water working."

The next day, before the seminar began, the president walked up to Mike and said, "You know, something amazing happened last night. When I made it back to my villa, I found that there was plenty of hot water. But that wasn't what was amazing. What amazed me was this: At 11:15, Hank knocked on my door and checked to make sure everything had been fixed to my satisfaction!"

That company president probably learned more from that one experience than he did at the advanced management course on how to get higher productivity. Why? He saw real mastery demonstrated in real life. He saw what was possible when a master, in this case, a master employee, goes way beyond his job description and sees a problem all the way through to its satisfying solution.

Summary

➢ Mastery is more than mere success. It is becoming better than the best.

➢ There are five equities that true masters develop and sustain:

1. Physical equity.

2. Intellectual equity.

3. Spiritual equity.

4. Psychological equity.

5. Financial equity.

➢ There are five areas of philosophy in which true masters strive for continuous improvement:

1. Metaphysics.

2. Epistemology.

3. Ethics.

4. Politics.

5. Aesthetics.

➢ Masters arise in *unexpected places.*

➢ Masters display *single-minded effort.*

➢ Masters don't get sidetracked about whether or not they're going to meet their goal. They know they're doing everything that needs to be done, and they keep on doing it.

➢ Masters know how to *wait for critical mass,* then act appropriately and without any hindrance.

➢ Mastery in your chosen field equals full attention to appropriate detail.

➢ Mastery doesn't come about if you don't take the time to develop it!

Profile: Mastery

Jack Nicklaus

Golfer and Businessman

Some stars are so bright you can see them at noon. There are those who believe Jack Nicklaus to be such a star.

Regarded by many pros as the greatest golfer ever to play the game, Jack has consistently thrilled spectators, duffers and presidents. Jack Nicklaus is a world record setter and a stimulus for creating entirely new categories of records.

Along with the six Masters Tournament jackets Nicklaus can wear as his mantles of success, he wears another mantle: that of being a model to people young and old who admire his accomplishments.

We believe that in order to bear the mantle of a master one must possess a set of behavioral standards that represent superlative internal values, coupled with the highest performance skills. Jack Nicklaus is such a master.

The early days

Mike first met Jack when the future golfing legend was a teenager at the First Community Church in Columbus, Ohio. Mike was the Minister of Youth and the Director of Camp Akita. Even in high school, Jack's actions were speaking louder than his words. His early golfing success had gained him quite a reputation.

However, it was clear that there was something special about him that was *not* part of his golf game. When Jack attended a youth group on Sunday evening at the church, others felt happy to be in the same group. The response he elicited had nothing to do with a "groupie" mentality, even though he was something of a celebrity at that point. Jack was low-key, a straight shooter, and expected no special treatment or recognition.

The reverend Tom Maurer, the associate senior minister of the church, said, "I wish there were more kids like Jack. He's a terrific example of what young men can accomplish if they work at it. I don't mean his rare talent in golf, but his fantastic attitude."

135

Although he was approachable, Jack gained an early reputation as a stoic, reserved person, someone who wasn't easily shaken. People were comparing him to a bear even in his high school days. Fred Learey, a friend of Jack's and a former associate of Mike's, said, "Jack's a grizzly bear with a big heart and a steady eye." The affectionate moniker "the Golden Bear" caught on as Jack became increasingly famous.

Mike's view of Jack as a young man was that he was a very special person. In spite of his early status as a golfing prodigy, he never came across as cocky or overbearing, as many young athletes do. He broke out of the box early by not falling prey to the customary "big man" syndrome.

Some time after Jack had emerged as a national star on the golf scene, Mike can remember how Jack's personal authenticity was demonstrated in his spontaneous responses to the fans around him in the stadium at an Ohio State football game he and Jack were attending. Jack smiled when fans called his name and spoke to person after person. He didn't look straight ahead and act as though he couldn't hear or see anyone, a classic (and transparent) technique often used by celebrities. It was Jack's ability to interact with others that set him apart.

Golf at Disney Studios

In the mid-60s, Jack came to Walt Disney Studios in Burbank, California, to take a look at the various projects Mike was working on relating to the development of Walt Disney World. Mike took Jack on a tour of his team unit in the animation building first, and Jack also looked at a preview of what would become the EPCOT Center. Mike explained the Disney working method and philosophy. A good businessman, Jack asked questions about the concepts behind the Disney organization's success.

Later, during a meeting with Card Walker (who was more interested in talking about golf than anything else), Jack said, "Most of all, I believe in mastering the fundamentals. You've got to really get your basics down and avoid looking for shortcuts." Card leaned forward in his chair. His own business philosophy was being espoused by the greatest golfer in the world.

Was Nicklaus's observation sound golf advice? Business advice? Advice on the art of living life fully and happily? We think it was all three.

Card told Jack, "It's those basics and fundamentals that count the most in our game, too. You know, you seem to concentrate harder than any person I've ever seen, Jack."

Jack smiled. "Yes, I'm always trying to improve," he said. "You have to be really honest with yourself about your own game if you want to improve it. I'm embarrassed by failure, but it stimulates me to try harder."

"Jack," Card responded quickly, "you're just like Walt. You're a perfectionist who's patient enough to keep trying, keep practicing, until you master whatever it is you've undertaken. There are some perfectionists who don't put in the practice time. That's one of those fundamentals you were talking about."

Jack nodded. "I practice best when I have something specific to prepare for. I really need a specific goal. I have to see a picture in my mind. The more clear-cut it is, the better I do."

This conversation between two outstanding men taught Mike several valuable lessons. He feels that he's never yet made the perfect speech or given the ultimate seminar. But he continues working on his "swing," adjusting his technique. He keeps polishing the fundamentals, working on the basics. That's a fundamental principle for anyone who wants to attain true mastery and break out of the box.

A trip to the Magic Kingdom

Mike's fondest memory with Jack was a trip to Disneyland that the Vance and Nicklaus families made together. Visitors to the park recognized Jack, of course. As the two families walked down Main Street toward Sleeping Beauty's castle, Jack's presence was causing a stir along the way. People were calling out to him: "Hiya Jack!", "Great Masters, Jack!", "You going to teach Mickey some golf?" And he was smiling and waving and returning their greetings without a hint of self-consciousness.

Mike's son Mark listened to the exuberant greetings for about two minutes, then he let go of his own dad's hand and walked up and took Jack's hand. Mike felt a tiny twinge of jealousy, but then he reminded himself that heroes are incredibly important—perhaps most important to young people. Besides, part of breaking out of the box is learning to keep your ego in check at the appropriate time.

It was a great day, one Mike's family will never forget. That night at bedtime, Mark said, "Dad, thanks for a perfect day. I'll never forget Jack. I had so much fun. How do you get to be a person like Jack Nicklaus?" Mark had begun the journey toward mastery by asking it. The answers are important, of course, but posing the *question* is the critical preliminary step.

Mark's question and Jack's example have motivated much of what Mike has done for the last 30 years. Both made a lasting impression on him.

Jack Nicklaus's Breakout Qualities

- Mastery
- Perfecting fundamentals
- Special goals sensed in detail
- Character
- Avoiding shortcuts
- Honesty with himself

BREAKTHROUGH TECHNIQUES

ACHIEVING EXCELLENCE

☑ Ask: Does the team have the proper discipline, the discipline of a master, that's necessary to achieve big breakthroughs?

☑ Are the team's five equities in order? If not, deal with issues up front.

☑ Utilize the five equities as cueing devices and forms of stimulus to help people think out of the box and achieve breakthroughs.

☑ Utilize the five major areas of philosophy as cueing devices and forms of stimulus to help people think out of the box and achieve breakthroughs.

☑ Seek out mastery in the desired breakthrough goal. Ask: *Who is it? What is it? Where is it? How can we tap it?*

☑ Stay with the project. Work it. *Keep* working it. Remember, the answers are out there if we just keep looking for them. Keep fishing for the trophy fish. Never give up until you have achieved mastery, achieved the Big Breakthrough!

CHAPTER 7

Achieving Constructive Goals

"An exemplary person of modesty and merit carries things through to conclusion."

—The *I Ching*

Long-term constructive goals are the pathways to the desired end results of our efforts. Our goals should reflect, and be consistent with, our values.

Constructive goals are goals that support life and further growth and development, as opposed to destructive goals, which suppress and curtail life. In this chapter we'll look at the best ways to support and follow through on constructive goals—life-supporting objectives rooted in solid values and standards.

Past, present, future

Goals excite and motivate people when they are tied to deep-seated values. Remember, though, that there are people who get so excited about long-term thinking that they can't focus on the present.

We see three types of people: the *pastist* (someone who dwells on the past); the *futurist* (someone who's always looking ahead); and the *presentist* (someone who lives for now). The work we're doing at the Creative Thinking Association of America is *presentist* work. We focus on what's happening right now in order to be able to project into the future.

Let's analyze the members of each of these groups in detail.

Pastists basically live in yesterday's memories. That's why they miss out on the present. To the pastist, the objective is to return to the old ways, the old outlooks, the old definitions, rather than to use them constructively to face current challenges.

There are people who make such a big issue out of conserving what *was* that they hold back what is about to be born. A pragmatic approach to tradition makes the most sense. Honor the past by building on it, not by following it blindly without thinking.

We should respect traditions, of course, but in a way that keeps us out of bondage to the past. Nostalgia is beautiful, as long as it doesn't inhibit us from seeing the beauty of the moment, from using our senses fully, from appreciating what is directly before us, the "existential moment." If we keep looking at where we've been, we may miss where we are right now.

What about the *futurists?* Actually, they render a valuable service. By looking ahead, they help others see where they are going. They make estimates, and they help others avoid potential problems. Isn't that what George Orwell did with his book *1984?* He played out a series of ideas about the possible abuses of massive government at a time in the then not-too-distant future. As a result, we now have a set of standards by which to gauge the effects of government intrusion in our lives—and a series of sober reminders about the consequences of overlooking issues like individuality, privacy and personal autonomy in our social arrangements.

Aldous Huxley accomplished something similar in his writings. Futurists like Orwell and Huxley take a look around the corner, paint a picture of what *might* happen and offer us some useful ideas on how to avoid the problems they saw. Mike lived near Dr. Huxley in the Hollywood area in the 1960s. He read and studied the works of the famous prognosticator with a passion.

When it comes to establishing long-term constructive goals, you need to do more than recycle old ideas or make predictions about the future. You have to be a *presentist.*

The present moment

Viktor Frankl, the gifted thinker and writer, spent years in the Auschwitz concentration camp during World War II. As a result of his experiences, he coined a term that is applicable to our discussion: the "existential vacuum," meaning that at the moment, in the *present,* there's *nothing.*

In his book *Man's Search for Meaning,* Frankl said that when he and his companions were in Auschwitz, he became so aware of the concept of the existential vacuum that it blotted out even the idea of escape. The *vacuum* was what compelled Frankl to summon his deepest resources for survival, to call on the most fundamental part of himself.

Yes, Frankl and his companions wanted to get out—the horrors of the environment they faced could hardly have left them with a desire to stay—but that desperate hope of escape was not the most important motivating factor. What motivated Frankl, what caused him to look into himself deeply, was the monumental task of coming to terms with the bleakness, the nothingness at the core of the Holocaust. That nothingness was bound into every moment. In other words, Frankl wrestled hardest with questions such as, "What am I going to do with the next three minutes? How am I going to make those next three minutes magnificent and truly worth living, even in this horrific environment?"

You may have heard an inspiring story about St. Francis of Assisi that's appropriate in this context. St. Francis, you'll remember, had such a gentle spirit that birds came to rest on his shoulder and animals came and gathered around him. One day St. Francis was out working in his garden with a companion who asked him, "If you only had 10 minutes to live, what would you do?"

And St. Francis turned to the man and said, "If I only had 10 minutes to live, I would keep on hoeing my garden." He appreciated the present and lived within it.

There's a parallel story in the Buddhist tradition. A great Zen master happened to be busy weighing out some flax on a scale. (Flax is the plant from which linen is made.) Someone walked up to the master and asked, "What is Buddha-nature?" (In other words, "What is true enlightenment?") And the Zen master responded, "Three pounds of flax." To the master what he was doing at that moment *was* enlightenment.

Neither St. Francis nor the Zen master were in an existential vacuum because they were finding the significance of the moment in their present activity. They were enjoying the beauty of an existential *presence*.

Living in the present moment. What an idea! Some of us plan for years to go on a trip to a particular destination. We save our money. We head for a Greek island, or to Las Vegas, or to play tennis at a top-notch facility, or to lose weight at a special spa, or to enjoy the warm, sandy beaches of a tropical island. Whatever it is, we go through elaborate plans to construct the perfect experience and end up losing sight of that sense of *presence*.

When we stop and think about it, do we place ordinary experiences among the highest moments of our lives? Usually not. But the highest moments, the peak experiences, the ones we remember for a lifetime, *are* the simple moments. Take this moment to remember some of your highest moments right now. Typically, these moments are not the result of weeks of preparation. They're just the result of actually being *present* in an exciting way, and that usually takes no preparation at all.

You're lying in bed with somebody you love. You're listening to a child read a new story. You're watching a sunset with your mother or father. You're gazing at the vibrant colors of autumn. These types of experiences only take minutes. They don't take years to plan. They don't cost anything. But they're the experiences we remember. Often, they're the most beautiful moments of our lives. Why? Because we weren't preoccupied with schedules and connections and objectives and revisions. We were just *there*.

Hoeing the garden. Weighing the flax. Watching a sunset with a loved one. They're the simplest acts in the world, and also, many times, the most satisfying. But only if we commit to them. Only if you give the next few minutes full value, like St. Francis did.

Please don't misunderstand. We're not saying you shouldn't have dreams, goals and plans. Everyone should! But the point is that those long-term constructive goals *arise out of* those moments of presence, those beautiful todays, those experiences of purpose and insight that are rooted in the present moment.

People who work toward long-term constructive goals know how to enjoy those precious moments, know how to use them for breakthroughs. Sometimes, in order to reach one of those moments, you need to withdraw and look at yourself for a while. Initially, this takes a certain resoluteness of spirit, but taking the time to contemplate yourself and your way of looking at the world is one of the most important steps you can take to become a *presentist* and to begin the process of setting and achieving constructive long-term goals.

The important thing is to have the courage to sit quietly with oneself long enough for a moment of presence to materialize.

A hallmark of mature people is that they can be alone.
They enjoy time by themselves,
And find satisfaction in their own company.
But being alone can also be lonely.
When our past crowds us with irreconcilable memories,
These memories produce worry.

Chronic worriers are merely rehearsing their troubles
Before they actually happen.
One way to reconcile irreconcilable memories is to review their causes,
And to plan for the future differently.

Resolve to take a new direction.
When King Arthur asked Merlin what to do in a time of sadness,
Merlin replied, "You learn something from it."
Worriers rehearse their troubles.
Resolved people plan solutions.
Whether we focus our thoughts today on troubles or solutions
Will determine the nature of tomorrow's memories.
Seek answers by thinking through the causes of problems.
Build the kind of memories you can be alone with tomorrow.

Finding a cause

When developing long-term goals bear in mind the importance of finding a cause that motivates you. There are plenty of causes that need supporters; this book isn't meant to help identify them. But whatever the cause you select, you must remember that a cause is best undertaken with conviction, passion and dedication.

When Mike was sent to Korea in 1950, he found a cause to take up. This cause—caring for orphaned Korean children—changed his life!

It was difficult for him (as it must be for every soldier) to leave the United States and face an unknown future. Mike had to fly overseas to South Korea, and then get on a train heading northward into -40°F weather on Christmas eve. The train was occasionally strafed by enemy fire! It seemed to take forever for the train to reach Seoul. He thought it was a tough ride, but every now and then the train would stop, and Mike would look out the window to see groups of little children begging for food. They wore rags. They were freezing and hungry. *That* was tough to witness and Mike felt compelled to do something about it.

Mike spent his first night in Korea traveling with a boy named Pak Sang Shil, a 13-year-old Korean who had seen his own mother, father and sister killed during the war. It was wartime, it was the dead of winter and yet Pak seemed to know exactly what he wanted to do, where he wanted to go and what he wanted to be, so Mike asked him for help in understanding the people of South Korea.

Mike and Pak came to a cave near the side of the road and Pak turned to Mike and asked, "Would you like to look in the cave?" Mike said, "Sure." So they got out of the car and entered a dingy cave. To Mike's complete shock, the cave was filled with small children. These children lived in the caves and usually only came out to beg for something to eat. Mike was probably one of the only Westerners to see one of these caves firsthand. In them, tiny children fended for themselves and even took care of infants!

These were the children of war. Mike still remembers them vividly; there is a picture of them in his gallery.

The entire experience troubled Mike deeply. He went to his company commander and said, "I think somebody here ought to start an orphanage." He said that the American spirit was a caring spirit, that it seemed contrary to that spirit to let children exist in such squalor and that somebody should do something about it.

First there was silence. Then the company commander looked at Mike and said, "Well, why don't *you* do it?"

Mike said, "I'm not the right guy. I just got here."

The company commander smiled and said, "No, it'll be okay. You do it. Just check in and get approval from the battalion commander."

Mike eventually got the approval, and he took on the job of starting an orphanage—a task he had no idea how to complete. So he tracked down Pak and asked him, "How can we start an orphanage around here?"

Pak smiled, looked Mike straight in the eye and said, "Well, the first thing to do is to get some orphans."

Pak and Mike found an abandoned Shinto temple on a hilltop in Seoul that would be a suitable home for their orphanage. The next thing to do was to pick the children. They could only take 100 to get started; 100 kids seemed like a good, constructive goal, given their resources. Mike and Pak got a Jeep and drove through the streets of Seoul and found orphans and brought them to the orphanage. For many of the kids who made it to the hilltop, survival became a realistic possibility for the first time in their young lives.

Before too long, there were five orphanages. Then 10. Then just about every outfit in Korea had its own orphanage. Because somebody, somewhere, had decided to do something about a problem. Somebody had managed to get past talking about or rationalizing a problem and had taken action to remedy it.

You need a cause to help you break out of the box. If that cause is part of your business, that's great. If it's something that doesn't reflect a for-profit mind-set, that's great, too. The key is to find a cause that will help people and commit to it.

Again, we don't need to tell you what your cause ought to be. You have to choose it for yourself. But choose something!

Controls

Another important requirement related to constructive goals is the ability to have effective management, or control, over plans as they proceed. There are four areas of control to consider: before the fact, during the fact, after the fact—and the final area of control, which is called *facing* the facts.

Before-the-fact control is based on forecasting, projecting and basically looking forward to the attainment of goals as they were planned. This type of control is closely linked to the establishment of standards. An example of an effective before-the-fact set of controls would be the decision to do research and to document your research during the time that you're explaining exactly what it is you hope to accomplish.

The second type of control takes place while an activity is going on: the during-the-fact control. The important factor to keep in mind is that during-the-fact controls give you the ability to make adjustments while an event is still going on. During-the-fact controls can take the form of a critical path analysis, or of diagramming, or of one-on-one supervision.

When there *is* no method of exercising control over a process during the time it is operating, tragedies often result.

The third type of general control, the after-the-fact control, is what clicks into place as we learn something from what was just experienced and gain new insights as a result. After-the-fact controls take the form of reports, meetings, analyses, reviews, evaluations, postmortem recommendations and even decisions to start over from scratch.

In each one of these areas—before the fact, during the fact and after the fact—there is a fourth type of control. This category of control applies to *all three* of the other categories, and it's called *facing* the facts. Facing the facts means avoiding what so many people do when faced with uncomfortable circumstances: engaging in "reality conversion."

What is reality conversion? It's what happens when we know what the facts are, but we convert them to suit whatever it is that we would like them to be.

One of the factors to keep in mind when we're trying to face the facts is the influence of *people and personalities* on our analysis. In fact, we recommend going through the following process when trying to implement before-the-fact, during-the-fact or after-the-fact controls with regard to your goals:

♦ Take the people out of the problem.

♦ Look at the facts.

♦ Make the decision.

♦ Then put the people and the personalities back in again.

The late Armand Hammer often talked about the concept of "uncoupling" problem situations, which means taking the problem apart, separating the pieces from one another and dealing with each in a step-by-step way. This process helps to remove subjective extremes that have been introduced by the participants in the problem situation.

People are often scared of this process because they don't want to face facts. They're more interested in the effect a situation will have on a particular person (usually themselves) than they are in the actual outcome of the control process. We *should* find out the specifics of the situation before attempting to factor in issues that may be strongly influenced by personalities.

The S-P-R sequence (discussed earlier in this book) stands for Stimulus, Pause and Response, and it has everything to do with facing the facts, rather than the personalities or other peripheral issues.

Some time ago there was a major airline accident in which many people were killed. After the accident, the cockpit tape was made public. If you listen to it, you'll hear reality conversion at work and be convinced of the lethal potential of engaging in this type of failure to face the facts. Three minutes before the crash, the pilot and copilot knew of the increasingly troublesome conditions before them. But tragically, they kept converting these pieces of data into a comforting and familiar pattern that was easier for them to deal with in the emergency situation. In other words, they rationalized the facts away. They told each other that the signs of danger would go away before too long. The result was a catastrophe that cost many people their lives.

The attainment of long-term constructive goals depends on paying attention to what's happening *right now,* by making the next few minutes count at full value and by instituting sound controls on all four of the levels we've discussed. When you don't implement effective during-the-fact controls, when you engage in reality conversion, you never get a shot at a long-term constructive goal. Tragedies occur. Slipups with the potential for wiping out entire businesses happen. These problems could have been prevented with proper during-the-fact controls.

As you think about how to set and achieve long-term constructive goals, consider the kinds of controls in place before the fact, during the fact and after the fact. You should have an idea of the factors that will help you recognize when a danger sign *isn't* going to go away. Know what steps to take to remind yourself of the importance of facing facts, of looking at circumstances as they are, of fighting off the temptation to convert reality into something it isn't.

3 types of goals

Our experience has taught us that people need three types of long-term goals to help them break out of the box. Ideally, each of the three goals should be present at the same time. Let's take a look at the three types of goals.

Personal goals

Typically, these are goals that relate directly to family or individual development. Some people might choose for themselves goals that tie in specifically to the idea of being a good provider to their children, perhaps by providing a better material environment than their mother or father was able to offer. How can daily activities enhance growth in this direction?

Vocational goals

One of our long-term objectives should be a vocational goal. We need to make the effort to remember an activity that captured our imagination when we were little, when we wondered what we would do when we grew up. One of our goals should reflect that dream.

Mike once met the president of a trucking company who had been a high school football star. This president, Ken Cook, told Mike, with a certain amount of embarrassment, "I've always loved flowers. But I never started a floral business, because it seemed like such a departure from my image at school." Eventually, Ken Cook, with the help of his friend, Red Scott, decided to start a chain of nurseries called Nurseryland, U.S.A. We were honored to be able to help them with the design of the nurseries. Cook converted his youthful dream into an adult vocation!

George Funk, the president of a potato chip company, told Mike that he had always dreamed of running a business that involved a new—for then—type of food called granola. He started a company called Funky Granola.

These men were able to take their dreams and turn them into realities!

Social goals

One of your objectives should be a goal that is tied into a larger social purpose. This goal should give you fulfillment as part of an ongoing effort to make the world a better place.

Lloyd C. Douglas called this type of goal a "magnificent obsession"—the kind of obsession that leaves people better for having come in contact with you.

Although it can serve as the model for any number of goals, the orphanage project is an example of a socially-based long-term goal. Mike and Pak attacked a problem head-on and made life more tolerable for many children.

The Repotting Cycle

Long-term constructive goals can be used to help us "repot" ourselves. We need to be able to plan for the next cycle of growth in our lives and move into new environments and find new opportunities. Perhaps you started out in one career or job that could be compared to a fairly small pot, and perhaps a few years later you found it wise to "transplant" yourself into another pot, one that offered you a little more room to grow. Many people feel stifled and constricted by what they do all day long. If that's the case with you, consider taking a look at your potting choices.

We're suggesting that you evaluate your next set of constructive long-term goals by *analyzing your past pot cycles,* and using information to plan your future repotting moves carefully. (The charts on pages 149-151 will assist you.)

By doing this exercise, and by looking honestly at your surroundings, you'll be able to determine whether, in your current situation, there's enough room for your roots to keep spreading out.

Repotting can be undertaken *entrepreneurially* (individually) or *intrapreneurially* (as part of an organization). It takes place as a process of personal renewal, not necessarily as a series of career shifts.

ARE YOU READY TO BE RE-POTTED?

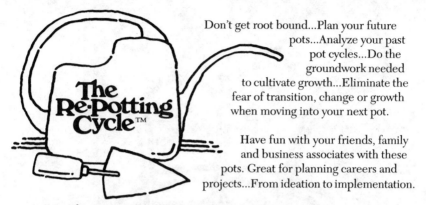

Don't get root bound...Plan your future pots...Analyze your past pot cycles...Do the groundwork needed to cultivate growth...Eliminate the fear of transition, change or growth when moving into your next pot.

Have fun with your friends, family and business associates with these pots. Great for planning careers and projects...From ideation to implementation.

Use This Easy Step-By-Step Approach for Planning and Cultivating: Continued Growth and Development, Career Moves, Life Cycles, Personal and Business Projects, Change and Transition.

Instructions:

1. Pot–A pot can be a new career, job, task, college, project or goal! For business and/or personal use. Applicable for all ages. Title your pot.

2. Age or time frame–From _____ to _____ . Enter when you want to begin this pot and how long you wish to remain in it.

3. Seeds, Skills and Dirt–List the skills, talents, attributes, qualities required to be in this pot.

4. Water/Fertilizer/Sunlight– Note what input, training and motivation, assistance or approval would be helpful and necessary in making the plant grow and flower.

5. Stems of Achievement–List your stems of achievement as they occur.

6. The Flower/Bloom–the result–achievement–accomplishment–product–conclusion–rewards.

7. Groundwork–State the necessary groundwork/foundation and elements needed to enter or move into a new pot for continued growth. (Having the necessary groundwork and foundation set can eliminate much of the fears of growth, change and transition.)

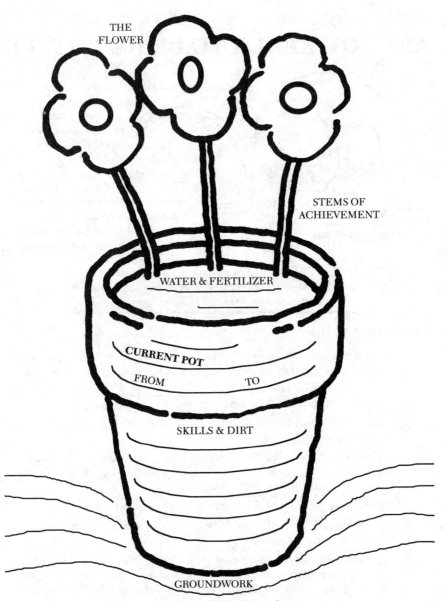

THE
FLOWER

STEMS OF
ACHIEVEMENT

WATER & FERTILIZER

CURRENT POT

FROM   TO

SKILLS & DIRT

GROUNDWORK

Causes For Diminished Performance:
•Staying Too Long. •Doing the Same Thing. •Achieved Goals
•Loss of Mentors•Not Using Cumulative Skills

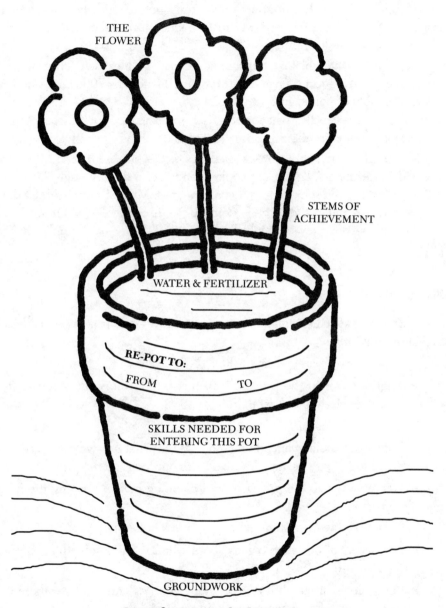

THE
FLOWER

STEMS OF
ACHIEVEMENT

WATER & FERTILIZER

RE-POT TO:

FROM   TO

SKILLS NEEDED FOR
ENTERING THIS POT

GROUNDWORK

Cures for Diminished Performance:
•Repotting •Replanting •New Vision •New Mentors •Full Use of Cumulative Skills

Why are many people rootbound? Why don't people change their pots more often? Because they're afraid of the transition. Preparation and groundwork are often necessary in order to make a smooth transition from one phase of our working lives to another.

Remember, though, that transitions are part of life itself! Not long ago, Diane was honored to be invited to Margaret Thatcher's 70th birthday party. There were lots of politicians, actors, philanthropists and other esteemed individuals in attendance. But what struck Diane was not so much the *celebrity* of the various people, but their inspiring ability to combine age with exuberance.

Most of the partygoers were in their 70s or 80s, an age that society associates with "retirement." Yet these people hadn't gotten that message. They were still contributing, still achieving, still goal-oriented. Most of them weren't doing exactly the same things they'd been doing 10 years earlier. They'd moved on to new situations, but they certainly hadn't retired. They had simply changed pots.

Summary

➤ Setting and achieving long-term constructive goals is an essential part of breakthrough thinking.

➤ Constructive goals are deeply linked with values.

➤ There's more to the process than just setting the values. You have to *follow* the values after you've set them.

➤ Living in the past has its limitations.

➤ Futurism—looking ahead to get an idea of what it is we may become—is all right, as long as it doesn't take away from our focus on the present.

➤ You're always in the present—and planning means bringing the future *into* the present.

➤ Existential vacuums translate to emptiness in the moment.

➤ An existential presence comes about when there is something *happening* in the moment.

➤ Being alone, although it takes courage, is an essential skill for those who wish to develop or refine constructive long-term goals.

➤ Attaching yourself to a well-selected cause is one of the best ways to focus on a long-term constructive goal.

➢ *Before-the-fact* controls typically result in sound forecasting, planning and research.

➢ *During-the-fact* controls allow you to have effective management over life as it proceeds.

➢ *After-the-fact* controls take the form of reports, meetings, analyses, reviews, evaluations and decisions to begin again from scratch.

➢ *Face-the-facts* controls underlie the other three, and this type of control means not engaging in "reality conversion," or the conversion of what *is* happening to what we wish *were* happening.

➢ By taking the people out of the problem, looking at the facts, making the decision and then putting the people and personalities back in again, you can remove subjective distortions from the control process.

➢ There are three types of long-term constructive goals: private goals, vocational goals and socially oriented goals. We need all three.

➢ Consider encouraging personal renewal by "repotting" yourself: analyzing where you've been and making the transition to a new outlook or approach to work.

Profile: Constructive Goals

Dr. Roy A. Burkhart

Minister and Author, First Community Church, Columbus, Ohio

Ohio Wesleyan University in Delaware, Ohio, once had compulsory chapel services three days each week; students had to attend or extra hours were added to their requirements for graduation. As a student at O.W.U., Mike had heard many outstanding speakers at the chapel services. (Truth be told, he had also missed a few when spring was in bloom on the campus.)

On one especially beautiful spring day, Mike walked by Grey Chapel on his way out of class. He wasn't planning to attend the service that day because Mother Nature was beckoning.

As he walked by the open chapel doors, he heard a voice coming from the pulpit—a voice that would change his life forever. He had never heard such a compelling voice. Mike stopped dead in his tracks. He wanted to hear more.

"The more you understand what you are, the more you understand others as they are. This is the first principle of all leadership: to start from where other people actually are rather than where you want them to be."

"Who is this?" Mike wondered.

What the speaker was saying sounded very different from anything Mike had heard before. His thoughts were unique in their content, and the manner and the style in which they were being spoken deeply aroused Mike's curiosity about this eloquent man. He couldn't pull himself away. The man speaking was nothing short of hypnotic. Mike noticed that others in the audience were just as attentive as he was.

"This is silly," Mike thought to himself. "No one is that powerful. It must be something in the air that's altering everyone's mood."

But when he looked again at the group, he realized that everyone—*everyone* — was in rapt attention, hanging on every word this man uttered. People stopped what they were doing to listen to this man speak.

Mike was so impressed with what he saw that, at the conclusion of the service, he went immediately to the university president's office, which was just across the hall. The president was Dr. Arthur S. Flemming, who later became Secretary of Health, Education and Welfare under President Dwight D. Eisenhower. Flemming was a man whom Mike liked very much.

Mike asked Dr. Flemming's secretary, "Who was that man speaking in Grey Chapel this morning? He was inspiring!"

"That's Dr. Roy A. Burkhart, Mike," she answered. "He's a very famous minister from the First Community Church in Columbus, Ohio. He's sitting at the desk in Dr. Flemming's office making telephone calls. Why don't you go in and say hello to him? It will be all right."

As he waited to go in the office, Mike reflected on other observations he'd heard that morning at the chapel service: "Man has sailed the oceans, soared faster than the speed of sound, explored the heart of the physical world and now is preparing to travel to distant planets and land on the moon. But he hasn't taken the time to explore the world within himself and to know himself. Now, all over the world, he prepares for the supreme adventure of all: the way by which a single person can fulfill an individual destiny. Remember, in all the world, no other person is like you. Just as there are no two blades of grass or leaves on the trees alike, so you are different from every other person who has ever lived, is now living or ever will live in the future."

Mike walked into the huge office of the president with some trepidation. Dr. Burkhart, who was seated at Flemming's mammoth desk, stood up and walked directly toward Mike. They shook hands warmly.

Mike said, "I'm Mike Vance, Dr. Burkhart. I loved your chapel talk this morning."

Continuing to grip Mike's hand, Dr. Burkhart responded by saying, "Mike, my boy, thank you very much."

They continued talking for a long time—about life in general, and about the fact that Mike was leaving soon for duty at Camp Polk, Louisiana, and then in Korea.

Mike couldn't possibly have known that the man with whom he was talking would be one of the most influential people in his life. He felt an almost immediate bonding with Dr. Burkhart, a connection that other people felt too when they met him.

He asked Mike, "What are you going to do with your life after you've completed your military service? What are you interested in becoming?"

"I'm interested in everything, Dr. Burkhart," Mike answered. "I can't make up my mind about just one thing."

"Why don't you come and work for me when you are finished with your obligation to Uncle Sam? You can do what I do," Dr. Burkhart suggested.

Mike, with a bit of uncertainty, asked Dr. Burkhart exactly what he did, anyway. He explained his work as a minister of one of the largest churches in America.

"You can be a minister, Mike," Burkhart assured him.

Mike laughed and said, "Well, I've got a long way to go before I could do that, including my military service. But I am interested in working for you. I read Dr. Harry Emerson Fosdick's inspiring book, *I Was Made a Minister*. It influenced me a great deal."

Mike and Dr. Burkhart—who was called "Burkie" by nearly everyone he knew—were soon fast friends.

The 7 Keys

Mike's relationship with Burkie was a source of strength during his service in Korea. His first Christmas away from home was a lonely experience. It was bleak, cold and dangerous. Like most other servicepeople, Mike's feelings were just about at their lowest point. The servicemen often sat around potbellied stoves trying to get warm in the frigid weather, but somehow they never felt warm enough. Mike decided that he needed to get warm from within. He thought about Burkie, who had given him a small printed explanation of what he called "The Seven Keys to the Kingdom." Burkie had scrawled a note across the top: "This will help you to get out of tough places. Love, Burkie." Here's the essence of Burkie's note to Mike.

1. The Master Key is Prayer—learning to think and feel in harmony with the universal mind, which is God. (Prayer is the process of making a request or petition to the Divinity.)

2. The Second Key is Faith—the capacity to trust. Burkie said, "Faith is reason grown courageous. It is a belief and trust in God's understanding." Faith is a guiding force in purposeful human endeavor for millions of people around the world.

3. The Third Key is Love—and this key lets the real self become an expression of the divine. (Love is often defined as the response to superlative values. People tend to love those who pursue values that they believe in deeply.)

4. The Fourth Key is Acceptance—by which you can actually create the climate of your own soul, by which you can actually make the events of life shape the high purpose of your life. (There are certain aspects of life over which a person has no control—being sent off to war, for instance. Yet, by accepting the experience, rather than resisting it, one can develop character and learn to set his or her sights on new constructive goals.)

5. The Fifth Key is the Key of Forgiveness—which is essential to winning complete freedom of thought and feeling. (People who never learn to pardon are forever in bondage to feelings of anger and thoughts of revenge.)

6. The Sixth Key is the Key of Healing—the key to a healthy body and spirit. (This key encompasses physical healing as well as the capacity to regenerate oneself spiritually.)

7. The Seventh Key is the Key of Total Commitment—the full giving of the self. (Commitment to a constructive goal can transform people into what God means for them to be. The ability to commit completely to appropriate goals is one of the greatest gifts of human existence.)

Mike found the Seven Keys to be a great reassurance during his tour of duty in Asia. Perhaps even more reassuring were handwritten letters he received at least once a month from Burkie. Mike reread these letters for inspiration many times during his service in Korea. He was moved by the fact that a busy person like Burkie would take the time to write to one lonely soldier. This reveals a quality that made many people revere him.

Here is a sample of one letter Mike received from Burkie:

The First Community Church
1320 Cambridge Boulevard
Columbus, Ohio

Dear Mike—
   You are in my thoughts and prayers every day. I have put a shield around you. I have faith in your return. Faith is reason grown courageous. By faith you can bet your life on belief in the wisdom and power of God, and it will not fail you any more than summer fails to follow springtime.
   You have every right to doubt and question. It is critical to doubt your doubts, to examine them and then in time you can come to a faith in your universe, in God and in yourself.
   You have to believe in the real you or you cannot know the real you. You will fulfill your destiny. I am thrilled over what God is doing and will do through you.

Always—
Roy

These letters helped Mike to remain steadfast and get through the many challenging months of combat duty. They also forged a bond between Mike and Burkie that could not be broken by anything.

Life changed abruptly for Mike when he rotated home from the port of Inchon, Korea. Within a few weeks, he went to visit Burkie at his church camp, Camp Akita, near Sugar Grove, Ohio. It was a joyous reunion.

Burkie immediately offered Mike a job at his church while Mike returned to college at Ohio State University. He suggested that Mike start by working with seventh- and eighth-graders and assume the general duties of a minister at his church. Mike was thrilled and excited to have this magnificent opportunity to work with and learn from Burkie. This was the beginning of a wonderful new life in which he would gain priceless knowledge about leadership and personal relationships.

Eventually Mike was in charge of the entire youth program of more than 1,000 youths, Minister of the Children's Church (Church of the Block of Wood), Director of Camp Akita, Founder of Youth on Call and participating staff Minister at First Community.

This is how Mike describes his time working with Burkie:

"So many things happened to me at First Community Church that it would probably fill two books this size if I described them all. However, the single most beneficial principle I learned was the value of committing oneself to worthwhile causes, committing oneself to help others and participation in charitable activities. My mother, Virginia, had instilled these principles in me, but First Community and Burkie gave them wings.

"Unfortunately, too many of us become self-centered to the point that we never consider the feelings or welfare of people around us, including our own families. We place the responsibility on society at large or the government. Fortunately, there are examples in daily life that show other ways to live. My own sister, Cynthia Titus, a full-time teacher for more than 40 years, cares daily for our ailing mother—defying the dumping-on-others principle.

"At First Community, we started a program for teenagers to learn the responsibility of caring for people. We called it 'Youth on Call.' It meant simply to be 'on call' to help other people. One of their projects was called 'The Church Helping Project,' where teenagers would pay pastoral visits to people who were shut-in or bedridden.

"This is how I met a woman named Marjorie Willock. She had been a first grade teacher in Columbus when she contracted polio. It left her almost totally paralyzed and confined her to a respirator for life support. We had young people from The Church Helping Project call on her once every two weeks for many years. Marge looked forward to these visits and became an inspiration to the young people. Experiences like this were enlightening and rewarding for the teenagers—and for the counselors, too."

Canadian fishing trips

Mike and Burkie had some unforgettable fishing trips in Canada where Burkie had a large cabin on a beautiful lake.

Fishing for bass with Burkie revealed a whole other side to the man, Mike felt. One morning they made a portage to a distant lake, hunting for a trophy bass. Others fishing in their party, including the church director of music, Lowell Riley, were using live spring frogs—spring peepers—as bait. Mike refused to use the frogs and stuck with artificial lures.

Finally, everyone was catching fish—big fish—except Mike. At last, Mike couldn't stand missing out on the fish any longer and rigged his rod with a hook, carefully placing a frog on it.

The instant he threw the line into the water, it was being pulled rapidly toward the center of the lake. Burkie shouted, "Let him go, let him go. Don't pull too soon." Lowell watched, having a good laugh.

Mike caught a beautiful bass, maybe five or six pounds, on his first frog. He had another frog on the hook before the others even got his first fish on the stringer. Lowell remarked that he'd never seen a frog get put on a hook so fast.

Burkie cackled with laughter. He said, "That's the fastest conversion I've ever seen. Mike, you're a believer!" And he laughed some more. That day Mike learned an important lesson about the perils of insisting on having his way. As usual, Burkie had helped make the process of committing to constructive change enjoyable, rather than traumatic.

Values

This then, was Dr. Roy A. Burkhart, who influenced Mike profoundly by exposing him to values that made him commit to constructive goals. Mike's favorite creation of Dr. Burkhart's is the benediction which he used to close his church services.

Mike says this Benediction out loud every morning when he gets out of bed, and recites it silently every night and before every speaking engagement.

Benediction
By Dr. Roy A Burkhart
And now,
May the courage of
The early morning's dawning,
The strength of the eternal hills,
The wide open fields, the silent streams,
And the beauty of the flowered gardens,
The love of the family,
The peace of the evening's ending,
And of the midnight,
Be with you now and forever.

Frequently, Mike also recalls Burkie's remarks on freedom as it relates to the mental formation of goals: "To find freedom is the first step in winning the freedom to become yourself. When your mind is free, you know who you are. When order is in your mind, there is order in your body, and you create order all around yourself. You need not be pushed around by thoughts, enslaved by thoughts, weakened by thoughts. Instead, you can be free to choose the thoughts of a person who knows who he is."

Dr. Burkhart's Breakout Qualities

- Loving and forgiving
- Personal and intimate
- Caring and committed
- Giving and trusting
- Encouraging and inspirational
- Showing deep belief in people

BREAKTHROUGH TECHNIQUES

ACHIEVING DESIRED END RESULTS

☑ Identify the type of goal you are striving to achieve.

☑ Respect the past, but don't get boxed in by it.

☑ Don't miss the moment. Don't let ideas slip by. Build on them.

☑ Practice the S-P-R (Stimulus-Pause-Response) sequence to improve responses to stimulus.

☑ Bring the future into the present by seeing what is possible.

☑ Don't let emotions get in the way of idea development. Deal with the facts. Take the emotions out of the situation.

☑ Utilize the Re-Potting Cycle personally and during team sessions to increase the likelihood of achieving meaningful breakthroughs.

☑ Use the "during-the-fact" controls to continuously update status.

☑ Work to achieve breakthroughs you can live with tomorrow. Will life be more malevolent or benevolent because of this breakthrough? Will this breakthrough have a positive effect? Can you be proud of it?

CHAPTER 8

Creating a Participatory Environment

"I ain't gonna work on Maggie's farm no more."

—Bob Dylan

Where do breakthroughs actually happen? They can happen anyplace, anytime. Breakthroughs happen more frequently if we set up a working environment that provides resources and techniques for stimulation. We call this type of environment "participatory."

This environment enriches people, challenges them and inspires them. It focuses more on creativity than on conforming, more on bringing people together than on keeping them apart, more on finding new ways of doing things than on reapplying the same "solutions" over and over again.

We know that creativity is stimulated by the inability of some people to follow rules that say how something is "supposed" to be done. Nevertheless, we can establish a participative climate that allows individuals to be free; free to be themselves, free to make a unique contribution.

Using didactic materials

How do you create a participatory environment? What is the guiding concept behind that design?

Maria Montessori, who founded magnificent schools to foster creativity, was famous for developing what she referred to as "didactic teaching materials." In other words, the materials themselves served as teachers; these were objects that a child could use and learn from independently.

For example, Montessori used objects intended to be touched and felt by a child. The very act of playing with these objects got the child to take a participatory role in the learning process. Montessori's ideas succeeded in much the same way as Walt Disney's workspace layouts did. These workplaces were filled with sketches and ideas placed all around the walls, encouraging employees to participate in projects from the moment they entered the space.

A truly participatory environment

As we discussed, these rooms are the Team Center, the lake in which people go fishing for great ideas. Such rooms are, to this day, where dreams are captured, planned, laid out and executed at the Disney organization.

The participatory nature of the room is the same as the participatory nature of Montessori's didactic learning tools. Both have a way of drawing people in, which is what any successful work environment will do.

The environment itself should be designed in such a way that it encourages participation and, as a result, breakthroughs.

Getting employee input

A participatory environment declares that we *want* to hear from other people. This is the guiding principle behind many of today's quality-first, listen-to-the-employees management philosophies. Sometimes, though, our ability to listen seems to be forgotten as we focus on so-called "bottom-line" issues—at the expense of other important matters. Participatory environments don't deliver results if people can't give meaningful input about the many ways to tackle problems and challenges.

Walt Disney nurtured a participatory mind-set in his organization through storyboards and team units. He once renovated a park attraction because a janitor pointed out some inaccuracies in the replication of a particular site. The janitor had lived in the area the attraction was supposed to represent; Walt hadn't. The changes were made.

The concept of the participatory workplace was, in large measure, developed at Disney. Much of it was later transplanted to Japan after World War II by people who had studied Disney's work. As Disney and a number of Japanese industries proved, a participatory workplace is *not* incompatible with a disciplined workplace.

An eyes-on experience

Our company helped design and build General Electric's Learning and Communications Center for the company's Transportation Division in Erie, Pennsylvania. The idea for the Center was created by a participatory environment set up in the work area of the General Manager, Rick Richardson. G.E. used the participatory process to design what would be its own participatory environment: the Team Center. Once it was completed, it was something to see. The walls were surfaced with cork or other materials to accommodate Displayed Thinking—a process permitting others to *see* what team members are thinking. Displayed Thinking is an essential part of creating a participatory workplace. It worked especially well at General Electric with Rick Richardson and his team. It worked because it was easy for everybody to track ideas.

Pictures are one way materials become didactic, one way they start to reach out and grab people. They appeal to our senses, and our visual sense in particular. Interest and participation in the workplace comes about when we make massive use of visual display—a high-visualization method that assures participation because of its didactic nature.

Using visual displays is an important technique that fosters breakthroughs in the workplace. It's a practical method for changing the environment, enabling it to reach out to people.

"Pictures representing ideas" is a concept that can be traced back to long before Walt Disney's time, of course. The ancient Egyptians used hieroglyphics on *their* walls to represent ideas and stimulate thinking. Leonardo da Vinci laid out pictures of what he planned to work on and incorporated those magnificent sketches of his in his notebooks. Then, in the 1930s, Walt Disney took the same concept, put pictures up on walls and originated what is now known as the storyboard approach. Later, we coined the term Displayed Thinking to describe our approach, which became our Creative Thinking System.

You've heard of a hands-on approach. Well, this is an eyes-on approach! Displayed Thinking is an eyes-on experience that lets you see what it is that you and others are working on. It's an enhanced version of a visual method of thinking.

Not long ago, we were working on a restaurant design project. The project was undertaken for Norman Brinker, founder and chairman of Brinker International. We put up 4' x 8' Displayed Thinking boards all the way around the perimeter of one of the two large rooms where we were working. We then proceeded to surround ourselves with visual stimuli—

images that would lead us to ideas on how we should design this restaurant. The results were remarkable.

Upon entering the room, the first feature we saw was a Briefing Board outlining the work to be done on this project. (You'll learn more about Briefing Boards later in this chapter.) As we went further into the room, we saw a summary of the philosophy of the company, the values it wanted reflected in its restaurants. Then there was a summary of the current trends, the facts one would need to know to operate a restaurant in the current business atmosphere. Next was a summary of all the relevant financial statistics affecting the project (i.e., how much capital was required to construct this type of project, what the break-even point was and so on). We had an entire Displayed Thinking area on possible names and themes, a profile of the target customers and the types of menu items the restaurant could offer. And as we made our way around we discovered other displays outlining training options and spin-off businesses that might arise out of the restaurant's operations, such as mailing list sales or catalog merchandising.

In the second room, we actually built scale models of the proposed restaurant. They were illuminated with theatrical lighting, and music played in the background. We designed the prototype table setup for the restaurant and served food items from the proposed menu. What an experience!

This approach, which used two side-by-side Team Centers, enabled people to go through the process of studying the ideas being displayed, become involved and then immediately *experience* the proposed restaurant atmosphere, complete with lighting, sound and food. The whole process took a couple of weeks to complete, but they were a well-spent couple of weeks!

These creative techniques delivered impressive results for us. They laid the foundation for a breakthrough. You can take advantage of the same techniques by putting together a participatory Team Center. Displayed Thinking will help you and your team break out of the box. A truly participatory environment employs Displayed Thinking to bring ideas into focus in a dramatic way.

How to make it happen

The participatory environment is an integral part of break-out-of-the-box thinking. It embodies the requirements for a people-first, inclusive, boundaryless culture. It doesn't have to be an expensive process, and it's a golden opportunity for a company to invest its money where it says its values are.

Implementing this kind of workplace is necessary if you want to get people involved. It's unrealistic to say, "We're all going to participate now," without changing the environment. You need a real, meaningful, didactic system that engages people, following the examples of Maria Montessori and Walt Disney as models. (See page 119 in our book *Think Out of the Box*.)

Step 1: setting up the room

How do you build a participatory environment from the ground up? First, select a team that you want to have work on a project, and help them get started on establishing the environment that will be the home and gathering place of projects. This process can be done at home or in your business. But the important requirement is training a team to work visually and to interact with visual stimuli that surround them.

In our seminars and training workshops, we teach people how to create participatory living and working environments. We call these environments Team Centers and A Kitchen for the Mind. They often become "headquarters" for business and home settings. A Team Center is a room equipped with Displayed Thinking boards for high visualization, as well as other resources and technology. A Kitchen for the Mind is a room in the home where one can develop "recipes for the mind." It contains such tools as books, computers and reference materials, and it helps focus intently on the development of new ideas. (We discuss the home-based creative living center called A Kitchen for the Mind in detail in our book *Think Out of the Box* and in our audiocassette program called *A Kitchen for the Mind*.)

Another way to understand the participatory concept when building one of these environments with your people is to think of it as developing an enrichment center. In an effort to improve morale, many companies are doing more to "enrich people." There are many company activities meant to provide enrichment, such as company bowling teams, softball teams, workout groups, fishing trips and golf tournaments. But along with this, we think it's essential to have a place in the building where people can go to enrich their thinking and make progress toward solving problems and designing new strategies. Design an environment that will expose people to the tools they'll need to meet the challenges they face in these changing times!

Start by selecting a space where people will be able to design a participatory environment. Then get a diverse team together. Try to make the group heterogeneous—composed of a wide variety of backgrounds and positions.

There's nothing more limiting than gathering together a bunch of vice presidents and asking them to come up with a strategy for saving the company. Their group perspective is too narrow to produce breakthroughs. (Besides, sometimes they believe their own press clippings.) Get people from a number of different levels and a number of disciplines. Mix it up. Introduce the CEO to the people in the basement.

The enrichment center also serves as a planning center. It should help people develop their own skills and abilities by using Displayed Thinking. Determine what other resources you want at your team's disposal and include them in your Team Center.

(Then why not take a photograph of the results and send it to us at the Creative Thinking Association of America? We'd love to see how it came out.)

Step 2: the Charrette

The second step takes place after you've built the environment and involves intense focus. Start schooling people on the requirements of a project under discussion. During this period, all the facts are gathered, background information is considered and the group takes some preliminary approaches that will eventually produce a workable solution. This process is known as a "Charrette," an intensive workout on a project using creative thinking techniques, including Displayed Thinking for high-visualization involvement. (The word *charrette*, common in architectural circles, originated in France.)

In a Charrette, decision-making is made incrementally, as the project progresses. Charrettes feature special kinds of briefings. These aren't meetings, oversight sessions or presentations, but "participations" in which the sanctioners, the people who authorized the project, interact with the team members. During the Charrette phase, senior people don't give approval or disapproval, but offer suggestions and take part in the process as it evolves. This exchange of information creates opportunity for consensus.

We recommend replacing presentations with participations as a *modus operandi*. Participations are the opposite of presentations and are essential elements of the Charrette, and interaction often fails without them. While presentations set the scene for a yea-nay, thumbs-up or thumbs-down outcome, participations encourage others to take part in the thinking process.

Interacting with top people during these step-by-step briefings creates some unparalleled opportunities for breaking out of the box! When the sanctioner walks in the door, not for an update but to take part in the work with the team members, the result is effective team-building that can lead to break-throughs. Mike was lucky enough to take part in this process at the Disney organization; when Walt Disney walked in to take part in a team's ongoing work, his presence built excitement and motivation. It also built a special kind of team spirit that has endured and has propelled the organization to the top of the entertainment industry.

It's important that project leaders find methods that assure members will work with the top people throughout the process. Although periodic participations are vitally important to the success of a Charrette, we recommend scheduling them for the entire life of the project, allowing the sanctioners and others to be involved in your team's efforts from the beginning to the end. This assures that you can benefit from breakthrough thinking that occurs at any time. And near the end of the planning phase, when recommendations are finally ready to be implemented, you don't hear the CEO of the company say, "Well, that's interesting, but it's not what I had in mind."

There are two additional suggestions to keep in mind about Charrettes before setting one up. First, they should take place at the early stages of a project. Second, it's difficult to achieve beneficial results when cramming a Charrette into a single day. This is particularly important, because attempting to make this all-important foundational creative work happen too fast reduces the quality of the research and development. In most situations, a one-day Charrette simply doesn't produce satisfactory results. There's too much pressure when trying to "wrap things up" arbitrarily, to get home before the traffic gets backed up or to prepare for the other meetings and reports that are due tomorrow morning. Schedule a Charrette for a two- or three-day period, and make certain upper management takes part by participating at key points along the way. (There will be top-level people who want to participate *throughout* the Charrette, not just at prescheduled times—which is even more helpful.)

Another point to remember: Breaks and refreshment times are essential parts of Charrettes!

By the way, Charrettes are an excellent opportunity to practice the creative thinking systems outlined in our book *Think Out of the Box.* These involve developing a *master plan* (an overview and foundation of project objectives), engaging in *idea development* (expanding on the concept or ideas of the master plan), using *communication* (making sure the necessary people are kept informed), setting up an *organization plan* (determining who'll do what and when), *retrieving* ideas that have not yet been used (checking the archives for good approaches that may have been overlooked), using a *Briefing Board* (setting up a during-the-fact control system—see the description of the Briefing Board below) and using *synapses* (bringing seemingly unrelated ideas into meaningful relationships). The acronym for all this is MICORBS.

Charrettes can improve the quality of your work, the speed of your work, the cost of solving problems and the level of creativity and originality people bring to projects or problems to be solved.

Step 3: the Briefing Board

The Briefing Board is a convenient and important didactic tool for guiding the activities of the participatory environment, a tool that Mike developed when he was Dean of Disney University. It's a critical and essential part of the creative process. The Briefing Board is the participatory environment's nerve center.

The Briefing Board is a during-the-fact control system. It consists of dated briefing cards divided into five major areas: Do (lists assignments that need to be done), Doing (lists assignments on which work has begun), Done (lists those tasks that have been completed), Hangups (lists problems of any kind and tasks that cannot be completed due to unforeseen problems) and Input (captures messages from team members to others in the group). (See page 170 for a sample Briefing Board and page 171 for examples of cards that can be used on the board.) Those are the five major categories, but feel free to adapt the system to meet your own specific needs.

There are many types of Briefing Boards: the personal Briefing Board that tracks the activities you're doing; the joint Briefing Board you share with an associate; the departmental Briefing Board; the company-wide Briefing Board; and last is the project Briefing Board, which is usually titled "Briefing Board for X Project." (Many companies like to jazz up Briefing Boards by adding special lighting and customizing the board to the particular needs of the company and/or employees.)

The effectiveness of the boards lies in their ability to get everyone involved instantaneously, with *visual* summaries of key events, projects and problems. It's all there in black and white (and color). Anyone involved with the work can add personal observations about potential obstacles in the Hangups column.

Companies that have many projects going on at one time set up a number of Briefing Boards at the same time and display them in a briefing hall, where employees can see the status of numerous undertakings at the same time!

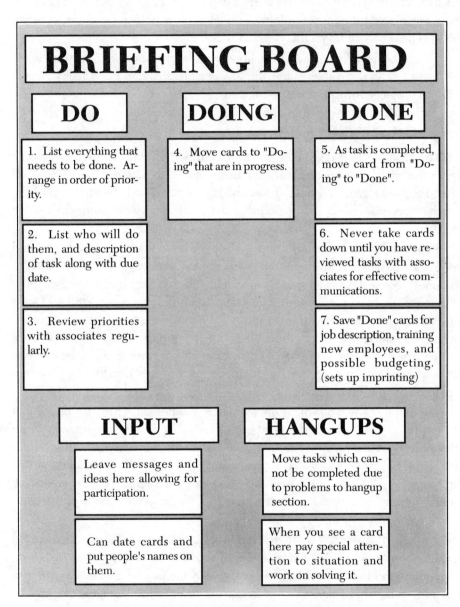

BRIEFING BOARD

DO

1. List everything that needs to be done. Arrange in order of priority.

2. List who will do them, and description of task along with due date.

3. Review priorities with associates regularly.

DOING

4. Move cards to "Doing" that are in progress.

DONE

5. As task is completed, move card from "Doing" to "Done".

6. Never take cards down until you have reviewed tasks with associates for effective communications.

7. Save "Done" cards for job description, training new employees, and possible budgeting. (sets up imprinting)

INPUT

Leave messages and ideas here allowing for participation.

Can date cards and put people's names on them.

HANGUPS

Move tasks which cannot be completed due to problems to hangup section.

When you see a card here pay special attention to situation and work on solving it.

© Intellectual Equities, Inc. 1996

Examples of Briefing Board cards

To:	Date:
Description	

From:

©MCMLXXXVIII Briefing Card

Due Date:

B R I E F I N G M E S S A G E C A R D ™	TO:	DATE:	TIME:	AM PM
	FROM:	PHONE: ( )		
	OF:	EXTENSION:		
	PHONE MESSAGE			

PHONED ☐ CALL BACK ☐ RETURNED CALL ☐ WANTS TO SEE YOU ☐ WILL CALL AGAIN ☐ WAS IN ☐ URGENT ☐

TO DO DESCRIPTION:

DUE DATE: FROM: **ie.** (216) 243-8015
©MCMLXXXVIII BMC

You can obtain Briefing Board cards and materials by contacting our office.

The Briefing Board is a tool that makes the environment truly participatory. Most companies update the Briefing Board daily to keep the boards current. The boards are also used for scheduling briefing sessions during the course of the day and are updated appropriately during the meetings. We have experienced very little resistance implementing this system because of its obvious benefits. People who might object to Briefing Boards do so because they're not comfortable with others knowing exactly what they're doing. However, this is rare. With a Briefing Board, everyone can know what's going on and that can be a big plus for your organization; and it costs very little to inaugurate.

Step 4: open meetings

Another concept used to nurture the participatory work environment is the open meeting. This is a technique that allows the organization to list *all* of the meetings for the coming month, as well as what departments or divisions they affect, who will be conducting them, where and when they'll be held, what the objectives will be and so on. Then *anyone* in the team can attend *any* of the meetings and take an active role!

The main benefit of the open meetings concept, besides inclusiveness, is that it helps the organization be efficient. Once a list of all the meetings that are going to be held over a 30-day period is reviewed and analyzed, redundancies and overlaps become obvious and streamlining is much easier. We have found that people who use open meeting methods are often surprised by the redundancy of many of the meetings that are scheduled!

At one company we work with, a kiosk—right in the middle of a corporate planning center in the headquarters building—lists every meeting taking place in the month ahead. Everybody knows what's going on within the company; everybody gets a chance to attend meetings and offer input. It's a creative idea that can make just about any work setting more productive and inclusive.

Obstacles to using these ideas

As we've learned, some team members may be uncomfortable with certain aspects of the participatory work environment because it's harder to cover up inactivity in these work environments. This makes for a strong argument when you're trying to convince management about the merits of the ideas laid out in this chapter. Establishing a participatory work environment helps to give everyone a better idea of what's really going on—and who is (or isn't) contributing to a project.

The principal reason leaders will drag their feet when it comes to setting up a participatory work environment is uneasiness about the possible negative effects of the change. They may be concerned about the access to sensitive information, for instance. To overcome this obstacle, implement appropriate internal safeguards, such as securing the facility so that only authorized team members have access to sensitive data, to prevent competitors or other unauthorized people from spying on your boards.

Others may resist adopting a participatory workplace because of concerns about a backlash if they don't utilize the recommendations and suggestions of contributing team members. To avoid a backlash, make it a practice to honestly spell out what is and is not going to be used.

Why Displayed Thinking works

Displayed Thinking helps you bring about a natural environment for participation. There are many ways to make it work effectively.

Why does using Displayed Thinking as part of a participatory environment deliver such tangible results? There are five major reasons.

1. The participatory environment works because it helps you operate at the speed of light.

Imagine you're standing in the center of a team room. You're able to scan the room and get an immediate sense of the key project elements. They're surrounding you. This is an "eyes-on" experience. One could say that you're working at a speed of 186,000 miles per second, the speed of light: the time it takes an image to reach you from where it is to where you are.

The speed of visual information makes it much easier for team members to respond quickly and intuitively. You've probably noticed that people are more likely to open up during group discussions that feature visual aids and brief, compelling written statements than they are during dry, "question and answer" sessions that have no visual element. The participatory environment takes full advantage of this more direct, involving communication style.

Buckminster Fuller, when reviewing the Displayed Thinking concept, said it all: "It's great. You can see an entire project at one glance!" He immediately understood the advantage of working with images rather than sitting people down for a traditional meeting. Words without pictures are less interesting and much slower than words with pictures. This way of working can reduce boredom, waste less time and money and get assignments finished faster.

2. The participatory environment works because of imprinting.

When you look around the team room, and scan the entire problem laid out from end to end, you are imprinting the information into your brain, just as you'd do when programming a computer. You are literally taking a picture of the information mentally, then storing the picture for later use. You do this by exposing yourself to information, facts, strategies and ideas that are laid out visually using Displayed Thinking. The idea is to imprint the information and retrieve it later by using the "triggering effect." The triggering effect retrieves ideas our subconscious mind has stored.

Who hasn't had the experience of trying to remember something and failing? For example, "What was the name of the 14th president of the United States?" You probably know that you've memorized this at some point in the past, but just can't recall it right now. But if you put the sentence "Franklin Pierce—14th President" up on a card and post it on a wall near where you're working, you imprint it.

Triggering and imprinting are valuable results from exposure to Displayed Thinking environments. Take advantage of them!

3. The participatory environment works because it uncovers new relationships between various parts of the problem.

As already discussed, the triggering effect allows you to retrieve information needed after you've been exposed to it in a Displayed Thinking environment. It also helps combine previously *unrelated* pieces of information in exciting new ways, and with virtually no effort, which is breakthrough thinking at its finest! This is called Grand Formatting.

Displayed Thinking systems bring together seemingly unrelated information into meaningful relationships. When elements come together coherently in this way, the result is *synergy*—the phenomenon in which a combination of elements is bigger than the sum total of the individual parts.

Synergy is one of the most exciting ways to summon breakthrough thinking—but synergy can't be forced. It arises out of connections that go beyond strict logic and rely, instead, on subconscious connections.

4. The participatory environment works because it reveals shortcomings.

When elements of a problem are laid out sequentially, you can take advantage of the presentation system's ability to imprint data directly into your mind and the connections between previously disparate elements become clear. You will then be able to notice gaps and oversights and missing pieces almost instantly. We call these missing pieces "black holes," and they're pretty hard to miss when you use Displayed Thinking boards.

When we spot a black hole during one of our sessions, we take a big piece of black paper and put it on the board where no one can possibly miss it. This piece of paper represents something that still has to get done.

This technique represents one of the most effective ways of avoiding the trap of reality conversion that we talked about in the previous chapter. When you spot shortcomings, don't pretend they don't exist, post a black hole. That makes ignoring the problem nearly impossible.

5. The participatory environment works because it's didactic.

When it's properly set up—with boards surrounding the entire room—a Displayed Thinking environment is virtually impossible *not* to interact with. Mike couldn't walk into Roy Disney's office without participating, in some way, with the challenge that Roy was focusing on at the time. The minute people enter this kind of work environment, they're taking part in the process.

In an environment that uses Displayed Thinking techniques by putting the facts, problems and resources into a visual setting, people respond! This is a compelling, all-encompassing way to get everyone engaged in the work. This kind of environment ensures and encourages participation.

The participatory work environment is one of the most powerful tools at your disposal for breaking out of the box and encouraging others to do so.

Set up your participatory environment today—and call us if you'd like assistance!

Summary

➤ Participatory work environments enrich, challenge and inspire people. These environments are often the settings for the greatest breakthroughs.

➤ These environments encourage employees to participate in projects.

➤ The participatory environment will deliver results only if you're willing to let people give input about the best ways to tackle problems and challenges.

➤ The participatory environment is an eyes-on experience that relies on Displayed Thinking, which is a *visual* approach to thinking about projects.

➤ In setting up the physical structures for your participatory work environment, get people from different levels and disciplines to work together.

➤ A Charrette is an intensive workout on a project using creative thinking techniques.

➤ Charrettes work best when they are conducted over a period of more than one day, and when the people authorizing the project are also involved.

➤ A participation is not the same thing as a presentation! The aim of a participation is not to get a yes or no answer, but to secure meaningful ongoing input to the creative process.

➤ Charrettes will almost immediately improve the quality of your work, the speed of your work, the cost of solving problems and the level of creativity and originality people bring to the table.

➤ The Briefing Board, a visual during-the-fact control system, is the participatory work environment's nerve center.

➤ An open meeting philosophy, in which all team members are welcome to attend all meetings, is another way to nurture a participatory work environment.

➤ When helping a superior accept a participatory work environment, highlight the fact that this environment will help the superior keep better track of the project, as well as identify who is and isn't contributing to key goals.

➤ Participatory work environments work for five reasons:

1. They help you operate more efficiently.
2. They help you take advantage of imprinting and triggering.
3. They help uncover new relationships between various parts of a problem.
4. They help identify shortcomings.
5. They are didactic. When correctly implemented, they're virtually impossible *not* to interact with.

Profile: Creating a Participatory Environment

Dr. Albert Suthers

Professor, Ohio Wesleyan University; Missionary, China, Korea and Japan

Mike learned a great deal from a remarkable college professor at Ohio Wesleyan University in Delaware, Ohio. The story of Professor Albert Suthers is almost like fiction to Mike today. Mike's memory of him always brings bits of wisdom, observations and profound knowledge when he needs them most.

When Mike first saw Dr. Suthers, he thought him the most unlikely person in the entire world to influence him. Mike first met Dr. Suthers as he entered his classroom one afternoon in Grey Chapel at Ohio Wesleyan. To Mike, he looked like a character out of a Charles Dickens novel.

His course, "Religions and Cultures of China, Korea and Japan," was not a hot item in 1949. World War II had just concluded and not too many people were interested in learning about these Asian countries. Mike remembers asking himself how on God's earth he had managed to get himself enrolled in a course on China, Korea and Japan that began at 3:00 in the afternoon—the time of day when everyone else went to the local hangouts. It was a time to be with friends, not a time to explore the religions and cultures of the Orient. And more to the point, how had Mike managed to get Dr. Albert Suthers—a former Christian missionary to China, Korea and Japan who looked like Ebenezer Scrooge—as a teacher?

Both of these immature questions would fade into the background as Dr. Suthers befriended Mike and the course became one of the best he ever had in his entire academic career.

The trunk

Dr. Suthers's classroom was an amphitheater-like room with very hard wooden chairs with squeaky cane seats. The environment looked worn, not unlike Dr. Suthers. Mike remembers thinking to himself, "It's going to be a long semester."

Even though the classroom could hold 100 students, only 10 students were taking the course. The small size of the class added to the starkness of the environment. A large, padlocked trunk in front of the professor's lectern caught Mike's eye. It added an ambiance of mystery to the room. Mike's curiosity was aroused.

When the clock struck three, Dr. Suthers finally spoke to the class. He introduced himself and said, "We will discuss the religions and cultures of China, Korea and Japan through the five major areas of philosophy. These are metaphysics, epistemology, ethics, aesthetics and politics. Before you is my trunk of artifacts from these three countries. We will study artifacts from each country from the contents of this trunk. By the end of the semester, we will have discussed every item in the trunk." He then walked over to the trunk, opened the padlock, removed it and lifted up the lid. Alfred Hitchcock could not have created more suspense than Dr. Suthers did that first day. He began to demonstrate his concept of "artifact teaching."

The first object he removed was a plate decorated with colorful, exotic-looking birds, strange forms and glorious peacocks. Dr. Suthers said, "This is my China plate; it represents the most populous country of the world. China covers an area of 3,691,500 square miles and has 4,000 years of recorded history. It's a developing country but seeks to be an advanced industrial nation someday. Confucianism, once the world's strongest religion, has been deprived of its metaphysical superstructures. Buddhism continues. Chinese mythology is rich with explanations for everything and provides China with an endless cultural history." The students were all spellbound.

Next, Dr. Suthers brought out a small box, slightly larger than a cigar box, covered with black silk. It contained clothing for a baby. The clothing was compactly folded, permitting it to fit into the tiny box. There was a pair of silk baby slippers, a silk pants bottom, a colorful top with silk black buttons and a silk robe. The students were amazed they all fit neatly into the black box. "This," Dr. Suthers said, "is my black box from Korea. It represents a Christmas legend practiced among Korean Christians. To greet the newborn Christ child, they laid out the clothing for the baby to wear. Korea is a tiny country but before the turn of this century it will be powerful. There is little uniformity of religious belief in Korea; some practice the Buddhist religion and others follow Confucius. Christianity is very new."

The third object Dr. Suthers showed the class was a wooden box about 12 inches long by 2 inches wide that contained tiny people made of wire and bead-like enameled heads. These, we learned, represented the 49 Samurai warriors of Japan who had each plunged a sword through their own heart to show allegiance to the emperor. Dr. Suthers said, "Japan is an island country of 143,818 square miles. It boasts a complex cultural life and its inhabitants practice Shintoism, Buddhism and limited Christianity. They, too, will be a major power by the end of this century."

Final exam

The Suthers artifact teaching method made for an ideal participative environment. The artifacts were didactic, drawing students into free-wheeling discourse, debate and an endless barrage of questions. The soft-spoken professor answered them all at his own slow, methodical pace.

The final examination for the semester-long course was nothing short of the work of a genius. On examination day, Dr. Suthers announced: "This will be an open-trunk examination. I have provided you with five blue books, one for each of the five areas of philosophy. There is only one question on the examination. That question is: Describe the meaning of the contents of my trunk in each of the five areas of philosophy for China, Korea and Japan."

"Teaching out of the trunk"

Anyone who has attended a Creative Thinking seminar knows that we employ Dr. Suthers's technique of artifact speaking and teaching. We have found it to be highly effective both for us and for our audience. We place our artifacts on tables at either side of flip charts as cues to us and demonstrations for our listeners. We use pictures, charts, diagrams, objects, models or anything conveying our point. We call it "Artifact Speaking and Flip Chart Tracking." We would like to thank Dr. Albert Suthers for his brilliant idea: "teaching out of the trunk" as a means of (literally!) breaking out of the box.

Dr. Suthers's Breakout Qualities

- ◆ Participation and involvement
- ◆ Involved learning
- ◆ Interest in students
- ◆ Thoughtfulness
- ◆ Dedication and devotion

BREAKTHROUGH TECHNIQUES

ATMOSPHERES FOR INVOLVEMENT

☑ Nobody has a corner on brains. Create an environment that allows others to participate. Add members to the core team. Get input.

☑ Have a working system, tools and materials that are didactic so others can see them, join in and understand what is going on without having to have a meeting or report. Make it an eyes-on experience. Allow for the triggering and imprinting effects to occur. Synaptic connections are easier to discover when you can see the big picture.

☑ Look for the black holes: shortcomings, omissions, missing parts.

☑ Conduct Charrettes (intensive workouts on the project) during the time frame of the project. Keep working on the project!

☑ Schedule participations: sessions when others participate on where you are on the project for accomplishing idea input and status updates. Bear in mind that participations are *not* presentations!

CHAPTER 9

Cultivating Mutual Respect

"A leader is a dealer in hope."

—Napoleon I

Randy was a member of an executive development group of which Mike was in charge at Disney Studios. He wanted to speak with Walt Disney about a major problem in his life, but he was hesitant about approaching Walt personally. He asked Mike for his advice.

Mike said, "I would encourage you to ask for Walt's help. He's never too busy to give someone support. Come on, I'll walk you down to his office."

Randy respected Walt deeply—probably more than any other person in the world—so it was with some trepidation that he walked into Walt's inner office, where the head of the studio was conducting a briefing. Randy said, "Walt, could I speak with you some time for just a couple of moments about something really important?"

Walt said, "How about right now?"

He excused himself from the meeting, and he and Randy disappeared into Walt's private office together. Here Walt took no phone calls and permitted no interruptions whatsoever out of respect for his visitors. Such thoughtfulness made Randy and everyone else respect Walt deeply.

Randy explained that his wife was dying from a rare blood disease and that he'd been unsuccessful in his attempts to get an appointment with the doctor who was the world's leading expert in this area. He thought Walt might be able to get through.

Immediately, Walt telephoned the renowned doctor. While Randy was sitting next to him, he secured an appointment for Randy's wife for the very next morning.

During his meeting with Randy, Walt's outer office was humming. Phone messages were piling up, people were waiting to resume meetings, visitors with appointments were waiting to talk about new projects. But Walt took the time to talk to Randy and help him out. He displayed respect for Randy. He extended regard, consideration and favor for Randy. Not surprisingly, Randy felt a very special respect for Walt in return.

Mutual respect is a key ingredient in establishing the kind of trust that creates a favorable climate for breakthroughs.

When mutual respect is absent, people become guarded and defensive, rather than open and forthcoming. If you want to develop an environment that precipitates breakthroughs, you have to find ways to cultivate mutual respect.

When you substitute controlling, authoritarian strategies for efforts to develop mutual respect, people you attempt to control will shut down. They may *look* like they're doing what you want them to, but in the end they'll be stifled. They either won't have breakthroughs or won't share the ones they do have.

Lao-Tzu, the founder of Taoism, said, "In governing, do not try to control." How right he was!

When Mike was in kindergarten, he had an experience that helped him understand the consequences of a lack of mutual respect.

As a young boy, Mike used to talk continuously about everything he saw or experienced. His kindergarten teacher handled what she viewed as too much talking in a harsh manner. She used an inappropriate "remedy" that had a negative effect on Mike and his relationship with her. She probably didn't mean to be harsh, but her response was a poor solution to the problem.

This teacher took a gauze bandage, dipped it in Mercurochrome and tied Mike's mouth shut with it. He remembers sitting in the corner, feeling humiliated. He felt hurt and afraid, as any child would in such a situation. And of course, the minute the teacher took the bandage off, he talked even more! The punishment helped to *reinforce* the behavior it was meant to eliminate. It simply accentuated a mutual disrespect, created hostile feelings and, ultimately, made the problem worse.

Punitive measures like the one Mike's teacher used don't usually bring about breakthroughs or solutions. They bring about rage, resistance and lack of cooperation.

What mutual respect means

Mutual respect means accepting each individual's right to be who he or she is. That is, you have to accept people's value systems, as long as those value systems don't hurt or infringe on the rights of others.

In cultivating mutual respect, begin from a position that acknowledges people's rights to self-determination, and see, as Thomas Jefferson saw, that people's ability to be what they truly are meant to be—to find their own path toward "life, liberty and the pursuit of happiness"—is one of the truths that make our magnificent social system work.

Motivated people would prefer to act and achieve on their own, or in co-operation with someone else, rather than to wait for a manager, a company or a government to act for them.

The concept of mutual respect is emphasized in Kahlil Gibran's book *The Prophet*. Gibran's work could really be considered a management book, and one of the best at that! *The Prophet* deals poetically with the ultimate management concern: deep values and how they affect us. In the book's section on marriage, Gibran observes that marriage is rooted in mutual respect. And a truly successful and effective work partnership should have some of the qualities of a successful marriage.

Often, what exists in the American workplace is closer to a *merger* between parties than a true *marriage*, at least as Gibran defines the idea of marriage. Rather than acting as a facilitator of breakthroughs, one person is chairman of the board and exercises authority and control over other people. That's neither a marriage nor a partnership. That's closer to a dictatorship.

A real marriage, one that reflects Gibran's famous description of the two pillars supporting the same temple roof, is the model to bear in mind as you pursue ways to increase mutual respect. Think of yourself as sharing in outcomes, as being married, in a way, to those whom you want to help break out of the box—and whose help *you* need for your own breakthroughs.

In a Gibran-defined marriage, the partners act as separate pillars, but have to be balanced perfectly if the structure is to stand. Separate, yet united. That's the kind of workplace "marriage" that leads to breakout thinking and builds *esprit de corps*. The ideas for breakthroughs presented in this book require achieving mutual respect, the same respect needed in a marriage relationship.

People can't expect anyone who doesn't respect them to encourage and facilitate breakthroughs. How can you hope to win cooperation, support and creativity from someone whose mouth has been taped shut? Stop and ask yourself: Are there people whose mouths I'm trying to tape closed? People whose ideas I'm not hearing out? People whose hunches I don't have time to explore?

We know of one executive who makes his managers follow an "open door" policy—and then shuts his own door for four hours every day, with a sign posted on it that says, "I want to talk to you, but not right now. Come back at 1 p.m." When his managers come back at that time, he listens impatiently to what his team members have to say, then brusquely dismisses them with a word or two! This isn't an open-door policy! It sounds more like a tape-and-Mercurochrome policy, one that will turn people off.

When you tell people you're operating by one set of rules but actually operate by another, you discourage respect. Bringing about mutual respect should not mean altering your normal work activities, but should simply encourage the maintenance of sound two-way relationships *while* you're doing what you normally do. Begin with respecting yourself enough to maintain clear standards and avoid self-deception.

Self-respect is actually the origin of mutual respect. If you grant yourself the respect you deserve, you'll attain that same respect among others. Developing and maintaining appropriate self-respect is an *ongoing* process. You have to continually devote attention to this important issue, because it can help improve your relationships with others.

Signs that mutual respect is thriving

When Vanessa Vance, at 7 years old, saw age spots on her grandmother's hands, she asked, "Grandma, what are those dark spots on your hands?"

Her grandmother replied, "Those are called 'aging spots.' "

Vanessa thought for a moment, then said, "Can't you just use some bleaching cream to get them off?"

Her grandmother laughed. "Well, maybe I could, but it so happens that I like those spots."

"How old do you have to be to get them?" Vanessa asked.

"People get them when they're in their 50s or 60s, usually," her grandmother answered. "Sometimes their 70s. You won't have to worry about getting them for a long time now."

"But can you ever get them earlier, Grandma?"

"What do you mean, honey?"

"I mean, can I get them *now?*"

"Well, why on earth would you want to do that?"

"Because I'd like to have them like you do now."

The next morning, Vanessa came to breakfast with tiny brown marks covering her hands. She had taken an eyebrow pencil and given herself her own "age spots"!

That's a childlike expression of mutual respect, and we think it's a perfect example. Real mutual respect can develop when one individual can identify fully with another—and Vanessa certainly identified with her grandmother! She wasn't alone. The very next day, Mike's son Johnny tried to pull out his own hair in one place so he'd have a bald spot just like his dad!

These are very poignant examples of mutual respect in the real world. When adults identify with one another with a tenth of that sincerity, mutual respect flourishes.

By sharing fully in the experiences of others, being involved with their experiences, rather than experiences related to your own priorities, you are on the way to developing a mutually accepting, mutually enriching way of relating to others.

Once you're *unmistakably* on the side of a fellow team member, mutual respect has the chance to thrive.

The casino of mutual respect

Mike was once called on to consult with the president of a large casino who was worried about the morale, attitude and customer service at the casino. He had pushed all the classic executive panic buttons—calling meetings, talking about budgets in a way that raised people's blood pressure, telling everyone to take half as long to eat lunch.

The casino had also commissioned an expensive study meant to determine exactly *why* morale and service were down. The report came back saying that the casino had hired too many "scuzzy" employees. According to the report, the casino staff's people skills were pitiful, their grooming was atrocious, their speaking skills were offensive, their body smells were noxious, their posture was frightful and their complexions would scare small children. The company's service problems were the result of a rude, unappealing work force.

The report concluded: "What you have to do is Disneyize these employees. You have to have a grooming policy, and you have to set up certain physical standards for them to meet before you let them interact with customers."

That is exactly what casino management did. It established meticulous grooming and personal deportment policies for 2,000 employees.

Can you guess what happened? The employees rebelled. They got mad. In fact, they got *furious*. They felt put down. The new policies only served to underline the fact that management didn't give any respect to the staff—the real underlying problem the expensive study failed to discover.

At about this time, Mike was invited to talk at a pep meeting for all the employees. Management asked him to talk about the "people skills problem" and to do whatever he could to resolve it. Mike felt as though he had been dropped into the middle of a war zone! (He joked with the president about doubling his fee for hazardous duty.)

Mike and Diane went to the casino and talked with the employees; they found the group warm, friendly and quite engaging. As a matter of fact, the report that the consultants had generated seemed to be describing an entirely different set of people!

During a group meeting with the employees, Mike mentioned something that he had observed about the work environment. He said, "Diane and I have made our own survey, and we've decided that the problem isn't you, the employees—it's your difficult guests! Let's face it—you've got customers who can be pretty testy! That's the problem! You guys are great!"

The employees stood up and cheered! The president gasped. The three or four management people sitting with the president stared at Mike in total disbelief when he made this remark.

Why did Mike make this remark? His approach was a simple one: How can you expect to get people to buy into your ideas if you tell them that they are second-rate people? Especially when they aren't? You don't succeed by saying, "We have a problem, and you're it, and would you please solve the problem?" That's inviting psychological and motivational disaster!

Mike's message to the employees was a straightforward one: "You're not scuzzy. This company hired you guys to work at this beautiful casino because its people thought you were great! Human resources said you were well-qualified, and we agree. It's the people *getting off the buses* we have to turn around. Have you taken a look at those people? They look like bulldogs! We saw them up there at the front desk—five deep, six wide, red in the face and ready to tear something apart. We need to find a way to straighten out those customers. But we have to do it carefully, and we have to do it in a way that doesn't blow up in our faces. What we have to do is implement a *courteous customer* program. We have to make a demonstration for those people on the bus, so they'll learn how it's done. And we have to lead by example."

Suddenly, the whole problem was shifted! Once the focus was on the customers, the employees responded immediately. They were motivated to show the customers a model example of acceptable behavior.

Mike's remarks about difficult customers—although they instantly gave top management a collective case of high blood pressure—were exactly what the staff needed to hear. Shortly after the talk, the group took a coffee break. What happened during the break out by the front desk demonstrated the power of offering people a touch of mutual respect. The employees didn't wait for someone to tell them what to do. They started getting together and talking about what they were going to do differently, right then during the break!

Immediately and on their own initiative, staff members began showing customers, by example, the most courteous service anyone could imagine. And that's not all. They started asking each other, "What can we do to make a courteous customer? What can we do to ensure such high performance that customers *can't help* but respond in a courteous way, even when they're difficult and irritable? What can we do that's so accommodating that it will turn around the attitude of *anyone*—even customers getting off the bus ready to fight? Show them respect first!" The employees started focusing on performing so well that the customers couldn't bring themselves to be irascible.

On their own, the casino employees came up with a startling plan for creating courteous customers: They got lots of people outside the front entrance, each with a clipboard and a handful of keys. That way, guests didn't have to wait in line forever to get a room key. By themselves, the front desk personnel found a procedure to help Mr. Smith get off the bus without incident. Someone was there to meet him, sign him in, take his credit card number, pass along a key and wish him a pleasant day. Mr. Smith was ready to have a fight over his room, as he had done in the past, but there was nothing to fight about! He became a courteous customer.

These ideas took root. They paid off. They spread to other groups of employees, including one of the nastier pit bosses, a man who was not noted for his sunny outlook. The technique worked out in the front lobby; it worked in other places, too.

The employees used the "courteous customer" concept to transform the casino completely. The personal communication, posture, hygiene and grooming standards got higher virtually overnight.

The task had changed from "clean up your act, employees" to "find a way to transform the customer into a cheerful one." That's what worked.

When you let the people on your team become the heroes, nearly anything is possible, because they'll be highly motivated to live up to the reputation you've passed along!

Shifting the goal and enabling your people to maintain their self-respect means not putting the onus on your own people. It means starting from a position of mutual respect. And usually, that's the *only* technique that works.

The supposedly substandard employees were building respect into their relationships with customers, respect that ended up coming back toward the employees again and reinforcing the entire cycle. It was a circle of mutual respect that perpetuated itself.

Success breeds success. Competency breeds competency. Mutual respect breeds mutual respect.

Those are the principles you should take advantage of. That's the operational strategy to use.

This self-perpetuating circle of respect helped turn the casino into an example for others. It went from being an average organization—one where managers pressed the panic button continually—to a highly profitable outfit. In fact, before too long, that casino was one of the six most profitable in the country! Why? The word got out!

By word of mouth, customers started hearing about how the company had reinvented itself by changing the way it dealt with people. The "courteous customer program" reversed the trend, and people started talking about that reversal.

This successful reversal would never have taken place if someone had walked in and started talking about how awful the employees in the casino were—how they lacked class, how they couldn't be counted on to maintain a top-notch business environment and how customers had a right to be treated better than they were being treated.

We can't habitually intimidate people and expect to be able to develop an atmosphere of mutual respect.

Do you remember the movie *E.T.*? The researchers tracked the alien down, and then, thinking he was dead, froze him solid. The little boy, Elliot, made his way into the cold storage area, where he practiced the finest management principle we've come across for helping people to break out of their boxes.

He said, "E.T., I love you."

Not "E.T., we've got a problem."

Not "E.T., this isn't going the way we'd planned."

Not "E.T., we're going to have to talk about some core principles together."

Not "E.T., there are going to be some changes around here."

Not "E.T., you're going to have to get up to speed with some new ideas."

He didn't say any of that! He just said: *"E.T., I love you."*

And E.T. turned out not to be dead after all!

When the chips were down at Chrysler, do you know what Lee Iacocca did? In essence, he said, "Chrysler, I love you!" Just like Elliot!

At another point in the movie *E.T.*, Elliot stood back and let E.T. develop the machinery necessary to "phone home." In much the same way, Iacocca stood back and let his dealers come up with innovative solutions to the serious problems that organization faced.

We've just seen superior breakout management concepts that represent entrepreneurism at its best:

> *Step one:* I love you.

> *Step two:* I let you.

4 principles for encouraging the development of mutual respect

There are four principles that help stimulate environments of mutual respect, environments that in turn support personal breakthroughs.

Principle #1: Uphold those successful people around you.

Uphold them! Support them! Don't put them down! And make a special point of supporting them when they succeed, too.

We have found that people tend to uphold the rights of the downtrodden more than the rights of the successful. A sense of balance needs to be maintained. Make a conscious effort to reinforce and support the people who are high achievers. Show support and encourage people in their accomplishments. Naturally, you should also respond to signs of problems. When problems come along, you should do something about them. But focus on the big picture, and that means keeping problems in perspective.

Support people without missing opportunities to take appropriate action to solve problems. Then you *exemplify* the proper ways to respond to those problems. (See Chapter 10 for a more detailed discussion of leading by example.)

Principle #2: Develop a trustworthy style that's appropriate for the occasion.

One trustworthy style is to train *everyone* to "think management." It means foregoing nepotism and political favoritism. And it means cultivating fairness among people above and below by committing to make integrity an unshakable principle in the working day—both in everyday matters, such as the scheduling of assignments, and in matters of greater long-term impact to the team. Train everyone to "think management" when a problem or opportunity arises. Train everyone to *take action* on the issue by getting it to the appropriate person.

Principle #3: Treat all people as VIPs.

This has been one of the most important ideas guiding the Disney organization: Treat all people as though they are very important persons. If you only treat some people as though they are VIPs, that actually brings the standards down all the way along the line. That's when customer service starts to get uneven. That's when vendor relationships start to get strained.

Every team member has something important to contribute. *Every* customer is worthy of full attention. *Every* supplier is an important partner in helping the organization achieve its objectives.

When management loses sight of these truths, the mutual respect is also lost. Thus, make a conscious effort to remind yourself of just how many VIPs you encounter every day.

Principle #4: Answer questions.

This may not sound like a major issue. But it's something that's remarkably easy to overlook in interactions with others.

If you hope to engender mutual respect, you have to answer people's questions consistently. We suggest that you set up a Displayed Thinking board in your workplace devoted specifically to the cataloging of questions that need answering. Usually there are many of them to address, and you can't be expected to answer every question *immediately,* but you should be able to answer most questions *eventually.* And when you do, you'll help people feel included and important.

Everyone has had the experience of being bombarded with questions. It can be overwhelming, but it is important to address all questions, whether immediately, or later, at a more appropriate time.

When you don't answer someone's question, you send the person the message that he or she is not worthy of your attention, and this isn't likely to engender mutual respect.

Where the water goes: a story about answering questions

One Saturday afternoon, a father and his son were on their way out of the house to go to a football game. The son saw that the kitchen faucet was dripping into the sink, and he asked his father, "Daddy, where does the water go after it goes into the sink?"

The father said, "Well, son, I can't answer that right now, because we're getting ready to go to the football game, but I'll answer it tomorrow." And at that moment he took a piece of chalk and wrote "where does the water go" on a chalkboard kept in the kitchen, a chalkboard devoted especially to recording unanswered questions.

The next morning, upon seeing the note on the chalkboard, the father took his son by the hand, sat him on the counter next to the sink and turned on the water. He explained how the water went down in the little hole through the little strainer. He shook some shavings from a pencil sharpener into that strainer, to show what it was for. Then he showed his son the pipes beneath the sink, and explained how the water flows through those pipes. Next, the two of them went down to the basement, and the father showed his son how the water worked its way through the bottom of the house and out into the street.

This father once told Mike, "When I was a little boy, my father never answered my questions. I asked my father that same question when I was a kid, and do you know what he said? 'Down the drain.' I remember going outside and crying because he would never give me a meaningful response when I asked him something. I promised myself that when the time came, I would show my children enough respect to try to answer their questions."

The story is such a compelling one that it reminds us of a wonderful book, one that we recommend highly, *The Inner Child of Your Past*, by Dr. W. Hugh Missledine. The entire book is about mutual respect, and it's well worth taking a look at. You'll read more about Dr. Missledine in the profile that follows.

Summary

➢ To develop an environment that precipitates breakthroughs, you have to cultivate mutual respect.

➢ Mutual respect means maintaining each individual's right to be himself or herself. Challenging that right by adopting punitive measures or asking other people to concede that *they* are "the problem" is counterproductive.

➢ Intimidating people will not develop an atmosphere of mutual respect.

➢ Mutual respect in the workplace is a lot like a good marriage: The participants are separate, yet united.

➢ Once you're unmistakably on the side of a fellow team member, mutual respect has the chance to thrive.

➢ When you let the people on your team become the heroes, they become so highly motivated that nearly anything is possible.

➢ Mutual respect means entrepreneurism at its best, entrepreneurism that says "I love you" and "I let you."

➢ The first principle for encouraging the development of mutual respect: Uphold successful people around you.

➢ The second principle for encouraging the development of mutual respect: Develop a trustworthy style that's appropriate for the occasion.

➢ The third principle for encouraging the development of mutual respect: Treat all people as VIPs.

➢ The fourth principle for encouraging the development of mutual respect: Answer questions.

Profile: Mutual Respect
_____

Dr. W. Hugh Missledine

Professor of Psychiatry; Director, Children's Mental
Health Center, Columbus, Ohio

Mike returned from the Korean conflict to become a minister at the First Community Church in Columbus, Ohio, famed for its work with young people. Dr. Roy A. Burkhart, senior minister, gave Mike the challenging assignment of creating a youth program for seventh- and eighth-graders in the church.

As part of that assignment, Mike was introduced to the eminent psychiatrist Dr. Hugh Missledine, who was a professor at Ohio State and director of the noted Children's Mental Health Center. Dr. Missledine would serve as a professional resource and adviser to Mike in working with the junior high school students.

Dr. Missledine advised Mike to allow the seventh-graders freedom to participate in the design of their own program, since this was the age when youth typically began to explore in their social roles. Coincidentally, when Mike conducted a planning meeting with a small group of seventh- and eighth-graders, they suggested having their own church just for junior high students—because the "big church," as they called it, was boring to them.

Dr. Missledine and Mike conferred about the unique idea, agreeing it provided a terrific vision for the kids. As a result of this meeting, The Church of the Block of Wood for seventh- and eighth-graders was born in Columbus, Ohio. It was housed in its own flagstone building on Lincoln Road and First Avenue in the village of Marble Cliff. Dr. Missledine had children of his own who became members of the little church, and this gave him an additional interest in its mission.

Mike's relationship with Dr. Missledine grew into a deep friendship as well as a professional association to provide guidance for the new church. The Church of the Block of Wood grew to more than 300 members rapidly. Mike attended many lectures of Dr. Missledine's, sat in on his seminars, studied his books and became a student of his teachings and child guidance techniques.

193

A very special relationship

Dr. Burkhart used to say, "Psychiatry is a study of the id by the *odd*." But this was not true in the case of Dr. Missledine! He was in no way odd, but rather a normal person with extraordinary insight into human behavior. He made abstract, often difficult-to-grasp psychological concepts easy to understand, and he showed others how to apply these concepts in real-life situations. His patients actually got better because of his skill and profound understanding.

The beginning of puberty is always a baffling time. This is true for parents and teachers of preteens, of course, but it is doubly so for the preteenager who is going through the process. Preteens ask, "What *are* these strange feelings I'm having anyway? What do I do about them?"

Far too often, people throw their hands in the air when dealing with junior-high-age kids, praying they will "get over it" soon—the sooner, the better. Not Missledine. His theory of the "inner child" provided insightful guidance and help for this challenging age group. His book on this subject, written in the 1960s, formed the basis for many other works on the "inner child" concept. Missledine was the originator of this concept that has circled the world.

A series of evening lectures Missledine conducted at the Minister's Seminar at the First Community Church was extremely helpful in Mike's work with the kids as well as in his personal life. Missledine's concepts about personality structure were quite simple compared to the complex theories of some experts, making them easy to apply to real life. Having responsibility for more than 300 puberty-ridden, energetic, sexually-driven, exasperated and often exasperating seventh- and eighth-graders requires group leadership skills that really work. Missledine gave Mike and the other counselors those skills.

The "inner child" concept rests on the idea that every adult consists of what he or she is now, what he or she wants to be in the future and, most important, the child that he or she used to be. Dr. Missledine said, "At some time, we were all children, but we often forget it in adulthood. We often try to ignore our lives as children, which causes much adult discomfort and unhappiness. Our little child still lives in us today, affecting everything we feel and do. Your inner child of the past lives on and must be understood. I am often asked how we should deal with our inner child."

Dr. Missledine offers three insights to help understand the "inner child":

1. The "inner child of your past"—the child that you once were—continues to exist in your life as an adult.

2. Being a parent to oneself matters. You already act as a parent to your "child of the past," whose reactions to your parental attitudes often create trouble.

3. Mutual respect matters. The basis of a good relationship with your "inner child" and with other people is mutual respect.

"Adult psychotherapy is essentially child guidance," Dr. Missledine says. "Our problems come from conflicts between our child of the past and our adult of the present. We must learn to be good parents to ourselves."

Dr. Missledine has helped people achieve further insight by his concept of the mature, healthy person vs. the immature, unhealthy person, psychologically speaking. He pointed out that everyone has common, basic drives—hunger, thirst, the need for companionship. Everyone also has *free will*, which is strongly influenced by the "inner child." Consequently, some people exercise control over their basic drives to achieve long-term constructive goals. Others, often those without constructive goals, let their basic drives take over and control their behavior. That is: they may eat too much, drink too much, become addicted to drugs or engage in other self-destructive behaviors.

Mike and the other counselors used both of these concepts, "the inner child of your past" and "the mature/immature person," at the church, and later Mike applied them in his Disney career. These two remarkable approaches have really helped people in personal growth and in the leadership of others. Mike is a strong supporter of and believer in Dr. Missledine's best-selling book, *Your Inner Child of the Past*, for further study in the area of mutual respect. It's an outstanding work that everyone should read. We offer the summary chart here as a stimulus for you to delve into the subject deeper.

"Your inner child of the past"
(summary chart given to Mike Vance at First Community Church lecture)

If your child of the past experienced:	What you can do about it as an adult:
Perfectionism and overcoercion	—Remove any excessive pressure and demands you put on yourself.
Punitiveness, perfectionism, rejection	—Put emphasis on being kind, respectful and gentle in the way you treat yourself; limit self-criticism.
Overindulgence	—Make reasonable demands on yourself to accomplish tasks; limit your over-dependence on other people.
Oversubmission	—Place firm limits on your impulsiveness; work to overcome your tendency not to respect the feelings and rights of others.
Neglect and rejection	—Intentionally do little kindnesses for yourself; indulge yourself when possible and decrease self-criticism.
Hypochondria	—Refuse to give in to your aches, pains and physical annoyances.

The death of Walt Disney

The death of Walt Disney brought considerable grief to people around the world because of his universal appeal and respect. Grief in the Disney Organization itself was overwhelming; the loss was a staggering blow that occurred right in the middle of the organization's biggest project ever—Walt Disney World in Orlando, Florida.

At this time Mike decided the Disney organization needed help in dealing with the intense sorrow and grief at a more professional level. He invited Dr. Otis Maxfield, a noted clergyman, and Dr. Missledine, to help everyone express their feelings and share their insights about effective leadership and supervisory techniques. They were both very effective in helping everyone deal with the sorrow and gave extensive ideas on enlightened management principles.

One management development group was working at the old, but charming, Hotel del Coronado in San Diego, California, on ideas and marketing promotions for a new concept called a "destination resort." Dr. Missledine was invited to spend a day teaching his concepts of the "inner child" and the "mature/immature person" to the Disney management team. These were highly productive sessions under the direction of Missledine, a skillful clinician.

Dr. Missledine said, "Your grieving for Walt is important and essential because of your intense feelings about him. I feel it also, and I didn't personally know him. It's okay if we weep together. However, we must also work through the idea that you can't worship a dead hero and fulfill your own potential. Likewise, we should not emphasize this to such a degree that we fail to maintain and conserve the hero's finer qualities. I would like to go around this room and ask each of you to express the feelings you are having about Walt Disney or something special about him that you remember."

The spontaneous service of memory for Walt that Dr. Missledine conducted that day was beautiful, serving as a catharsis for many pent-up feelings. It taught Mike and others who participated to talk about, rather than withhold, emotions. Later, Mike and several other Disney team members walked along the beach in front of the del Coronado Hotel with Dr. Missledine, watching the golden sun sink into the Pacific. And as they had dinner together at the Marine Room, right on the beach in nearby La Jolla, California, waves splashed against the large plate glass windows and the ceiling rolled open to reveal the night sky with the stars shining through. As they stared silently into infinity, Mike and the others knew that they were going to be all right...and that Walt was, too.

The importance of camaraderie

This fantastic experience taught Mike about the profound importance of socializing with people—especially a person like Hugh Missledine—who help shine a light on the true insights that can be part of everyday experience. Most of the time, people are in too big of a hurry to notice what is meaningful in life. They miss those special moments that prepare their minds and hearts for creative breakthroughs. When Mike and the others spent time with Dr. Missledine on the beach, they were able to nurture and truly *experience* the moments that faced them, which is vitally important in both good times and challenging ones.

We encourage our clients to take the time for these special occasions. We encourage them to get close to people and build some comradeship with their team members, to dream about the future, to grow closer—and to follow the example set by Dr. Missledine in cultivating mutual respect.

Dr. Missledine's Breakout Qualities

- Respect for others
- Kindness and gentleness
- Openness and honesty
- Ability to simplify complex concepts
- Ability to empathize with others
- Love and concern

BREAKTHROUGH TECHNIQUES

ESTABLISHING TRUST, OPENNESS AND HONESTY

☑ Conduct a powwow session with the team. (This idea is detailed in our book *Think Out of the Box*). Powwows reveal people's hidden skills, talents, values, needs and goals. This will help bond the team and uncover any incompatibilities among team members.

☑ Establish rules and/or guidelines to engender mutual respect for team members. How will you deal with hostilities? Do you trust one another? Respect for others' ideas leads to breakthroughs.

☑ Remember: United, you create; divided, you destroy.

☑ Uphold people's ideas; don't disregard them. Breakthroughs are stifled if you are doing creative thinking and analytical thinking at the same time. Do analytical thinking at a designated time.

☑ Don't ignore people's questions. Write them down. Acknowledge them. Decide when you will take the necessary time to answer them. Don't stop the flow of the project.

☑ Uphold and honor those who are successful. Don't assume that people who routinely do good work don't need reinforcement.

☑ Let people become heroes by treating them as such. Ask: *What will I do to treat everyone as a VIP?*

CHAPTER 10

Managing by Values

*"Decision-making is easy when you know what
your values are."*

—Roy O. Disney

Roy O. Disney, chairman of Disney and Walt's older brother, was often asked about the secret behind the company's unequaled success in the entertainment industry. He would always respond by saying, "We manage by our values, because decision-making is easy when you know what your values are."

Are values always positive in nature? No! Any person's existing code of conduct may be basically *constructive*—for example, "It is wrong to take things that don't belong to you"—or basically *destructive*—for example, "Sometimes you have to be willing to break the rules if you expect to get ahead in this world." Constructive values tend to support and uphold life; destructive values tend to destroy and put down life. Constructive values support a healthy climate that fosters breakthrough opportunities. Breakthroughs, discoveries that dramatically improve the quality of our lives, simply do not occur where there are values that distort the truth or hurt others.

Breakthroughs happen when one discovers big truths. Thomas Edison used to say, "I didn't *invent* anything. I *discovered* things. The answer is out there if we keep looking for it."

It's time to look at the last of our 10 strategies for breakthrough thinking. This one may just be the most important tool for breaking out of the box: managing by values.

We think that a global movement toward management by values is going on throughout the business world today.

Values are the principles by which one decides how he or she is going to live. Values produce the standards that influence and guide behavior. Standards, in turn, translate values into goals and objectives. Because our values produce the principles that guide us, it may be easiest to think of them as a code of conduct, one that we follow on a deep, even intuitive basis.

We know one man who grew up in a household where, during tough times, family members constantly said things like "We never took handouts from anybody, and we're not going to start now." In that family, self-reliance was an important value. Another family we know of meets every challenge and obstacle with the following attitude: "God will help us overcome this." In that family, religious faith is an important value.

Such values guide personal and family lives. They also have a big impact on interactions with others on the job. But as Dr. Mortimer Adler, the philosopher, author and editor of *Great Books of the Western World,* argued so often, you can't really *teach* values to people by talking about them. Lecturing someone about what is or isn't ethical is usually ineffective unless the ideas are demonstrated by the actual behavior of the person hoping to act as a role model. Teaching by talk alone cannot replace actual experiences that demonstrate the preferred behavior.

You can *demonstrate* a value, and you can *act* according to a value in such a way that your commitment to it influences other people. You may be able to win a certain amount of lip service from people by attempting to impose values on them externally, but you certainly shouldn't expect commitment from them unless you find tangible ways to put the principles into action in your daily life. In the end, embracing a value is an action you must undertake on your own. By the same token, while *instilling values* is tough, remaining committed to them may also be tough.

Values and decision-making

Constructive values lead to *more* effective use of the resources at your disposal, and destructive values have a way of leading to *less* effective use of them. As a result, destructive values lead to very poor decisions.

Louis Lundborg, chairman of the Bank of America, said, "Values that need explaining are usually the ones that people are having trouble maintaining." He might have added that values that *aren't* being maintained usually result in decisions that are less than our best.

When constructive values are well-defined, decision-making becomes easy.

Borrowed values

If you examine your attitudes closely, you may find that you haven't truly embraced the values by which you claim to be guided in making decisions. For example, if you *say* that your guiding value is "treating the people with whom you work as partners" but then scorn every idea that they have, it may be time to do some thinking about exactly how thoroughly that value has been incorporated into your real-life interactions.

In other words, you may *borrow* the value because it sounds good. Implementing it, however, so that it guides your decision-making, is a different matter. That takes time, practice, a willingness to be honest with yourself and commitment to the value.

Borrowed values lead to mediocre decisions—at best! In trying to act on values that have been imposed by others, you won't go through the same steps that led another person to adopt those values. Unless you come to the same conclusion about it as the other person did, in the end you will probably either reject the value or merely pay it lip service.

When values are embraced as the result of a conscious choice, they make perfect sense. However, when they're not, they fall into the category of "secondhand values."

In managing your organization, keep the following in mind:

◆ The greater the correlation between individual values and the company's objectives, the higher the potential for achievement and breakthroughs will be.

◆ The greater the correlation between individual values and the company's *perceived* objectives, the more effective the use of resources will be.

When values are clearly established, management by values is simple. You know what the values are, so you know where you want to go in the long term. The result is greater achievement.

There are many kinds of values that affect us: personal, peer group, family, school, church, company, country and so on. One of the approaches we recommend when it comes to management by values is to develop a "values profile," which allows you to set up a detailed summary that identifies your values in each area. In our cassette series, *Management by Values,* you'll find a detailed summary of the process by which you can conduct what we call a valuing session.

Management by values doesn't replace management by objectives. But if you don't know what another person's values are, it's going to be hard to develop enough mutual respect for the two of you to attain *any* objective together.

Using values to precipitate sound thinking about the situations you face is one of the best ways to break out of the box! Breakout thinkers are constantly coming up with new ways to apply their deeply held constructive values to shifting circumstances.

Productivity is a value-driven process

Managers who focus only on the bottom line miss out on their chance to affect the "top line"—the factors, such as values, that *determine* the financial results. Our value structure is the cause; the bottom line is the effect. Strong values lead to strong financial results!

There's nothing wrong with being concerned with the bottom line, but there's probably nothing worse than a management style that focuses *exclusively* on the bottom line! Effectively managing an organization means focusing on the cause—the values—as well as the effect—the bottom line.

It has become a trend for many organizations to draft value statements. However, value statements can sometimes be very superficial and perfunctory, and this can have a negative effect on productivity. To be meaningful and effective, a value statement should truly reflect an organization's practices. It should not be composed of buzzwords that really mean nothing in an organization's day-to-day activities. For example, if your company's value statement is: "We want people to be involved, because we're a company that believes in people," there has to be a system for accomplishing the aim embodied in that value. Just *saying* that you believe in this value will accomplish nothing. In fact, it may harm your organization, because professing a belief and not abiding by it will erode people's trust in and their commitment to your organization.

When they are not believable, proclaimed values can make people cynical about what you're trying to accomplish. The value only works if it is exemplified *before* it is put down in writing. When talking about values, be open about what you have and haven't accomplished yet.

Steve Jobs, a man who has made a habit of saying exactly what he thinks, once looked at a carefully crafted written statement of Apple Computer's values and said to us, "That's awful!"

He meant that when these values were placed on paper, they looked and sounded just like everyone else's: "We care for people," or "We have a passion for quality," or "We love our customers." He and Mike Markkula wanted a value statement that could be exemplified in employees' behavior.

"We care for people!" Yes, but we have to *show* we care for our people, rather than just talking about how much we care for them.

"We are committed to excellence!" Yes, but we have to make a specific, impossible-to-miss contribution to higher quality, rather than just talking about how important high quality is.

"The customer comes first!" Yes, but we have to update our technology so that it's easier for people on the front lines to stay informed and take full responsibility for a customer's needs, rather than just talking about how much we love our customers.

Values are, as we discussed in an earlier chapter, most powerful when they're translated into standards and creeds for the organization to follow. But we have to be sure, as we're setting the standards and circulating the creeds, that we're not drawing people's attention to a collection of buzzwords and clichés that are, as Steve Jobs would put it, "awful"!

A lesson about values

One day, a young mother visited the great Indian spiritual and political leader Mahatma Gandhi during a period he'd set aside for public audiences.

The mother had come in the hope of winning Gandhi's help. She put her young son in front of the most revered man in India and said, "Sir, please talk to my little boy. He eats too much sugar. I want you to look him in the eye and tell him that it's time for him to stop eating sugar."

Gandhi thought for a moment, looked at her and said, "Come back and see me next week."

The woman left, and a week later she was back in front of Gandhi again during his public audience period. She said, "Sir, talk to my son now. Tell him how important it is for him to stop eating sugar."

Gandhi looked at the boy and said, "Your mother is quite right. You must stop eating sugar, just as she instructs. Will you promise me you'll do as she says?"

The boy looked up, wide-eyed, and nodded his head yes.

The mother looked at Gandhi and said, "Thank you, sir. But may I ask why you asked us to wait a week to pass along this instruction? You could have told him as much when I saw you the last time."

"When you saw me the last time," Gandhi said with a smile, "I had not yet stopped eating sugar." While this may be a legend, it nevertheless teaches the importance of taking personal responsibility for a value.

The importance of taking responsibility for a value is also demonstrated in the following story. During the construction of Walt Disney World, Mike was walking around the site of the park with Roy Disney. Roy saw a sign on a Disney trailer that said: *All vendors must report to the lobby*. He stopped, stared at the sign for a moment and then said to Mike, "Take a look at that sign. Read it to me...How does that sign make you feel?"

Mike read the sign out loud, thought for a moment and then said, "Well, not very good, actually."

Roy said, "That sign reflects the opposite of what the Disney philosophy ought to be. I wonder how that sign got up there."

What Roy was really saying was, "I wonder who's in charge of teaching philosophy around here?" The point was not lost on Mike, who was in charge of teaching the Disney philosophy at the time!

Right then and there, Roy not only had the sign changed, he had the whole *approach* to dealing with so-called "vendors" changed so that it reflected Disney's people-first values. Roy saw to it that these people had a special reception area set aside just for them, one where the dream of the unfolding park would become as clear to them as it would to any of the organization's employees. He saw to it that the representatives who were coming to the site to supply or sell goods and services were treated like the valued partners they were.

Roy Disney, like his brother Walt, knew that in order to attain breakthrough levels of performance—both individually and on the organizational level—focusing on constructive values has to be an indispensable *first* step. He knew that constructive values have to govern decision-making, not follow along behind them. And he knew that constructive values had to start on a personal level before they could be extended throughout an organization.

Fake values

Some time ago, Mike attended a party in Palm Springs. He noticed what appeared to be a full-scale war going on by the poolside. Now, you don't often see full-fledged confrontations develop between adults who are chatting next to a swimming pool during a party, but that's what was taking place. A woman Mike knows was in the middle of a heated argument with a consultant about a political candidate the consultant represented.

What was the cause of the fight? Eventually, Mike found out. The consultant had shared his opinion that it really didn't matter what the candidate in question *believed*. Mike's friend had said something along the lines of, "What do you mean, it doesn't make any difference what he believes?"

"It's irrelevant what he believes," the consultant had explained. "What we do is commission polls and study trends and follow public opinion. So we *tell* him what to believe." Well, that's the remark that started the war. That consultant very nearly got tossed into the swimming pool! When people assume fake values—values that arise out of the Chameleon Complex—there is usually trouble.

The consultant probably had never heard about constructive values. If he *had* ever heard about them, it seems clear that he only thought about them for long enough to tell the people he worked for to discard them! That's the Chameleon Complex—the *opposite* of management by values—in action. *First* you figure out what people want to hear, *then* you determine exactly what it is you stand for. How does it work out in the long run? Not too well for the candidate, whether or not he's elected (and heaven help him if he is). And not too well for the people he represents, either.

Chameleon thinking is not thinking at all, and it's certainly not to be confused with management by values. Chameleon thinking leads to bad decisions, bad organizations and, of course, bad government. We advise that you avoid chameleon thinking for the simple reason that it's not an approach that leads to breakthrough thinking. In our view, any politician who is so bankrupt of ideas and principles as to be willing to try to fashion a career out of the Chameleon Complex deserves to inherit every problem the democratic process can serve up.

And by the way, values are not reserved for managers. At many successful companies today—Microsoft comes to mind—the alignment between any employee's personal outlook and the mission of the organization is, generally speaking, so strong that employees at *all* levels have learned to distinguish the issues that are worth raising a fuss over.

At today's most successful companies, high values (and high standards) are part of the culture, part of the basic quality orientation of the company.

You probably know why this happens. Working within a set of high, constructive values is more *enjoyable* than working within a set of low, destructive values. Shoddiness is stressful. Incompetence is stressful. Dishonesty is stressful.

Constructive values, on the other hand, lead to work that may *sometimes* have stressful periods, but that leaves you feeling fulfilled over the long haul. Which type of work would you really rather perform?

Your management-by-values program

We'd like to suggest that you develop a *management-by-values* program. (Refer to the chart on page 207 for a review of this and other leadership styles.) But remember that the vast majority of great management ideas fail to take root because of overemphasis at the beginning and lack of follow-through later on.

We're suggesting a *gradual, long-term* approach to building and reinforcing constructive values in your organization. This could mean spending less time in meetings and more time interacting with people one-on-one. It could mean setting up an enrichment center that helps to highlight important values within your company. It could mean finding ways to take personal *action* in accordance with a particular value at least once a week—and keeping to that schedule.

These ideas offer better options than lecturing people, or trying to "sell" your team members on a new idea or a new way of doing tasks. You can probably come up with any number of other creative ideas on your own for accentuating constructive values over the long term.

Take it a step at a time. Don't oversell it. Don't present the value you've decided to embrace as the be-all and end-all of your company strategy. Keep an eye out for a single element that needs changing, and then work from there.

Thousands of people in hundreds of organizations have benefited from the management-by-values approach by thoughtfully implementing change, picking battles selectively and demonstrating values, one situation at a time.

Talking about values is easy, but it doesn't work. Demonstrating values a step at a time takes more skill, and it also demands a certain knack for knowing what to demonstrate when. But it works!

The Value Spectrum

Management Styles

Old Style	Transitional	New Paradigms	Problems of Transition
Authoritarian Management	Management by Objectives	Management by Values (constructive)	Values must be clearly understood, not trumped up
Told what to do and how to do it	Participative (some say in policy formation, management remains central)	Participative and facilitator leadership (strong voice in policy formation and day-to-day operations)	Time-consuming, especially when old meeting format used; need new work environments (Team Centers)
Control, direct, dominate	Support, uphold, help, assist	Facilitator, provide tools, respond to the needs	Should not stop giving ideas and suggestions about direction (polemics)
Dictate	Criticize	Analyze	Easy to get buried in details (briefings)
Risk-taking by upper management and owners only	Small business units, decentralized, accountability, paper entrepreneur	Entrepreneur and intrapreneur design	People not really getting money, rewards, profits; not handling risk
Throw people in, sink or swim	Hype people up, push them to achieve	Self-motivation and genuine positive environment (Maslow)	Hype only lasts a short time and must be repeated often (celebrations)
Absolute policies	Free form	High standards but loose/tight	People flounder for a reference point and need of standards
Total bottom-line operation	Bottom-line approach tempered with respect for top-line	Top-line thinking; cause behind effect	Miss the passion of being cause-centered
Men only	Women accepted	Women key players	Men threatened, defensive

Homework

Demonstrating values applies not only to our offices, but also to our homes. The same "show-it-rather-than-tell-it" idea we've been discussing applies to our interactions with those we love; it can achieve wonderful results with children, who, as we already know, usually don't react well to lectures.

The idea isn't to *trick* our family members into accepting our values, but to take the opportunity to *implement* constructive values a step at a time, together. Eventually, you will find that you, your children and your family members will be paying deep attention to constructive values—together. This is a breakthrough worth achieving in any relationship!

Summary

➤ Values are what we consider to be important enough to act upon.

➤ Values produce the standards that influence and guide our behavior. Standards, in turn, translate values into goals or objectives.

➤ Borrowed values lead to mediocre decisions at best.

➤ The greater the correlation between an individual's personal values and the company's objectives, the higher the potential for achievement and breakthroughs will be.

➤ The smaller the correlation between an individual's personal values and the company's *perceived* objectives, the lower the potential for achievement and breakthroughs will be.

➤ Exemplifying values is much better than talking about them.

➤ Constructive values lead to work that may have stressful periods, but that leaves you feeling fulfilled over the long haul.

➤ Thoughtful, step-by-step implementation of values is likelier to be successful than an all-at-once approach.

Profile: Management by Values

Louis Lundborg

Chairman and CEO (retired), The Bank of America

The telephone rang in Mike's office at Disney Studios. It was Roy Disney.

"Mike, an old friend of yours is here in my office, Louis Lundborg. I'm trying to get some more money out of him," Roy said jokingly. "He'd like to drop by to see you on his way out of the studio this morning. Are you free?"

When the CEO of your company calls to tell you that the chairman of the Bank of America would like to see you, you're free!

Louis Lundborg had befriended Mike when he was a guest on Mike's Los Angeles television show *Men at the Top*. In fact, Lundborg was one of the most interesting and inspiring business leaders to appear on the one-hour program. Lundborg seemed in many ways to fit the mold of the bank chairman—he was urbane, distinguished and an impeccable dresser—but he was truly one of a kind. Unlike many top financial executives, Lundborg was unusually friendly, warm and quite forthcoming.

While he waited for Lundborg to arrive, Mike recalled his experiences with his old friend and ally.

Mike's show, *Men at the Top*, featured business executives and others who had made it up the ladder of achievement. Mike worked to launch the program because he believed that there was more to success than simply working hard and knowing the right people. What was each successful person's philosophy on personal achievement? Mike wanted to explore this topic in depth.

Mike developed the show under the auspices of an organization he had started called the Future Executives of America. The show's format included four outstanding college students who questioned and interacted with the featured guest each week.

To get the ball rolling, Mike needed commitment from some impressive leaders who would appear as guests. Otherwise, he was going to have trouble persuading

NBC's program executive Jack Keniston to give him a chance. Mike thought to himself, "What I need to do is to book one of the most powerful and influential leaders in all of Los Angeles. Who would that be?"

He consulted with a friend of his, a prominent insurance executive named Leon Saliba. Mike trusted Leon's judgment implicitly.

Together, they came to the conclusion that the ideal first guest for the show would be the chairman of the Bank of America, the world's biggest bank. It sounded like a pipe dream, but Leon encouraged Mike to go for it.

With considerable timidity, Mike phoned the Bank of America headquarters in Los Angeles, asking for the chairman, Louis Lundborg.

Mr. Lundborg listened to Mike's nervous explanation about the proposed program. At the end, he said, "Mike, I like the basic idea for your show. I like your values. I like the idea of exposing outstanding college students—and the audience—to people who have succeeded, and I like the idea of discussing *why* they have succeeded. I like the concept of getting at basic values, the principles people truly believe in. And I particularly like the idea of college students conducting the interview, rather than professionals. So, yes, I'll appear on your show."

The secret wall

Mike's reminiscences were interrupted by the appearance of the genial Lundborg at his office door.

"Good morning, Mike," Lundborg said, smiling. "I'm so glad to see you again. It's always too long between our visits. Roy tells me the Disney management development programs are going very well. He's pleased with the progress being made defining the values of the Disney Way of doing business. He thinks you'll earn your pay this month." And the banker winked.

After catching up on old times, the two men engaged in a vigorous discussion about the "secret wall" in the Disney management development center. The 30-foot-long wall, concealed by a curtain behind Mike's desk, used cards to illustrate the values that guided important business decisions at Disney. It was an essential group tool for creativity that allowed for the free-ranging—and often anonymous—posting of ideas. (The "secret wall" is discussed in greater detail in our book *Think Out of the Box*.)

Lundborg was taken by the idea, and said that he was going to try to develop a wall that did the same thing at the Bank of America. He asked Mike if he might contribute ideas for the wall in the area of decision-making, which is a challenge to everyone in leadership or management positions.

Together, they wrote ideas on 3 x 5 cards to place on the boards. They called the summary...

The Lundborg principles for making decisions

According to Louis Lundborg:

"I ask myself two basic questions when trying to make a decision about an issue. First, what are the *best* and the *worst* things that can happen if I do what I'm contemplating on this issue? Second, what are the best and the worst things that can happen if I do not do what I'm contemplating on this issue? Then I apply those two questions to five major areas.

1. "How will the decision affect the bank?

2. "How will it affect our customers?

3. "How will it affect me?

4. "How will it affect my family?

5. "How will it affect my country?"

These Lundborg Principles became part of the Disney Way for many young executives who were preparing for future leadership in the expanding Disney organization. Because the questions probe at fundamental values, they proved to be effective guidelines for many at Disney over the years. (We regularly apply the Lundborg Principles in our work at the Creative Thinking Association of America, and we find them particularly worthwhile in keeping our thinking value-focused.)

After their discussion about the Lundborg Principles, Mike asked Mr. Lundborg whether he would consider talking about Bank of America's "best practices" to a group of Disney executives in leadership development courses. He agreed. This effort became an early example of "benchmarking" between two collaborating companies.

Lundborg was a visionary, a man 30 years ahead of his time. He was a trailblazer among major "establishment" players, encouraging senior management to get "with it" on social issues, employee participation and loyalty to customers, employees and the community.

Loyalty to employees is a principle Lundborg strongly believed in. At one lunch meeting, Lundborg reminded a Disney development group of the words of Andrew Carnegie.

"As you become leaders in the Disney organization," he said, "remember what Andrew Carnegie said: 'Take everything from me and leave me my people, and I'll rebuild.' Be loyal to your people and they'll be loyal to you. Don't worry about *your* promotion. Worry about *your people's* promotions. Zealously protect the relationships between the Disney Company and your employees, because ultimately, your employees will determine your future success or failure. Yes, sometimes you must trim expenses. But do it to everything else *before* you do it to people. Cutting your people should be the very last resort. When we build insecurity and lack of trust in our people, it always comes back to haunt us. It goes directly to the bottom line."

Perhaps Louis Lundborg should conduct some management seminars on basic training for executives today.

Downsizing and outsourcing has, in too many instances, become a substitute for creativity and finding new solutions to changing work patterns. These days, "leave me my people" would certainly be a refreshing call to action by some enlightened CEO. In fact, we think the heroes of tomorrow's business success stories will be those who maintain their human resources by creating new career concepts.

Understanding people

One evening after dinner at the California Club, Lundborg had an enlightened discussion with a group of Disney people for several hours. His ideas made a lasting impression on Mike. "In leading and managing, we have to remember that everyone is insecure—but everyone is insecure about different things. We have to understand what insecurities we're dealing with to avoid stimulating an unnecessary crisis that hurts people," Lundborg said. "This is why slogans and clichés should not be used as a substitute for thought. Silence may be more productive when we don't know the situation.

"The business world is always changing. Things are always in flux. The problems of a new house or a new building begin when we move in. Only the truly ignorant ignore detailed thinking about the moving-in phase. Your inimitable founder, Walt Disney, understood this concept. He devoted equal amounts of time and money to the *people part* and to learning just how a new facility will operate. When this planning is being done only as construction is nearly completed, you're dealing with a poor leader who is interested merely in the facade. We must *look at* the people in the situations we face, not just put labels on them."

Christmas at Disneyland

The holiday season is a special time at Disneyland, a season honored with many traditions: beautiful decorations, parades, special events, unique sounds, smells and sights. One of the most important tradition involves choirs.

Each year on the Sunday before Christmas, choirs from all over California are invited to sing in a concert in Disneyland's town square. The choirs form a huge living Christmas tree as tall as the Main Street train depot! A full symphony orchestra plays a stirring program, and Christmas scriptures are read by a guest celebrity.

Mike invited Louis Lundborg and a number of others who assisted with the benchmarking program to attend this beautiful event as a thank-you from the Disney Company. Following the ceremony and concert, Lundborg and the other guests attended a private party in the Trophy Room at Club 33, above New Orleans Square.

During the evening's discussion, Lundborg told the guests, "There are three vital issues that corporations must come to grips with in the near future. They must produce and deliver products and services at high quality with a market-acceptable price. They must conduct their businesses in a way that is fair to employees, customers, suppliers and the environment. And they must become sensitive to the problems of the total community and do something to help resolve those problems. And they must be lead by action, not lip service!"

Liberty

The Bank of America headquarters building in San Francisco, California, is a stately structure that affords a magnificent view of the romantic city it occupies. The chairman's office on one of the top floors offers a particularly breathtaking panoramic look at the City by the Bay. Mike often visited Mr. Lundborg there to get advice and to talk philosophy.

The last conversation Mike had with Louis Lundborg had to do with the chairman's personal concerns about America. Lundborg said, "The most important thing of all is liberty. That's more important than profits, taxes, dividends or wages. Liberty ensures our freedom of expression. And education gives us the knowledge to express our convictions.

"Education should build character, but not by forcing old values on the young—rather, by exposing them to the best values and thinking of all ages and offering them a choice. Truth will win out.

"We must raise the baseline higher when we're determining what is acceptable human conduct. We need more integrity!"

Mike can recall standing in the street after this visit, looking up to the top floor of the Bank of America building, thinking that he had shared time with a man whose values were as high as the building where he worked. Lundborg, he thought to himself, is an out-of-the-box thinker.

Louis Lundborg's Breakout Qualities

♦ Support of important causes

♦ Commitment to community service

♦ Staying contemporary

♦ Willingness to take unpopular positions

♦ Continuous study and learning

BREAKTHROUGH TECHNIQUES

ACHIEVING TOP-LINE THINKING FOR BOTTOM-LINE RESULTS

☑ Are your decisions easy to make? If not, check your values to see if they are compatible.

☑ Are you practicing the Chameleon Complex? (In other words, are you telling people what they want to hear?) Or are you truly working to achieve a breakthrough?

☑ Are the values yours or are they borrowed from someone else?

☑ Do you truly believe in the breakthrough, or is it the conclusion of someone else's thinking?

☑ Are you doing top-line or bottom-line thinking? Great top-line thinking will usually lead to breakthroughs, which will in turn produce a great bottom line.

☑ What's the goal? How will you know when a breakthrough has occurred?

☑ What will be your measurement of success for the breakthrough?

☑ How will you implement the breakthrough?

Some Final Guidance on Achieving Breakthroughs

That's it. You now have 10 effective tools you can use to stimulate breakthroughs on your own and in your work with teams. Here's a brief review of the ground we've covered in this book.

10 principles for breakout thinking

1. **Unlock your ability.** Maintain the Life Cycle of Learning.

2. **Establish standards that reflect your values.** Be sure that your standards reflect constructive objectives, so your breakthroughs will be based in reality.

3. **Get work done through others while having fun!** You'll be glad you did.

4. **Design a creative environment**—A Kitchen for the Mind in the home, a Team Center within a business. Maintain a creative climate and culture where breakthroughs can occur continuously.

5. **Motivate yourself and others.** Put yourself and others on the "streetcar named desire." The breakthroughs are out there—if we keep looking for them.

6. **Master your thinking process.** Embracing the concept of mastery means more, is more fun and is *easier* than "just getting by." When people challenge themselves to do something the best that it can possibly be done, their minds open up and breakthroughs occur.

7. **Achieve constructive goals.** Choose goals that uphold what is most important to you. Define your long-term constructive goals and objectives so that your breakthroughs will hit the target—bull's-eye!

8. **Create a participatory environment.** With today's technology, the power of the individual is awesome, but participation and collaboration strengthen us even more.

9. **Cultivate mutual respect in your relationships and teams.** Teams perform at high levels when an atmosphere of mutual respect is the foundation.

10. **Remember that effective breakthroughs come from a clear set of values.** When goals and objectives are compatible with constructive values, breakthroughs occur—and are implemented—more often.

These 10 breakout principles will make you a revivalist. As you go through the seasons and cycles of life, you'll be equipped to meet the inevitable challenges you encounter if you follow these 10 principles.

Vicarious breakthroughs

The creation of the lovable character Mickey Mouse was a breakthrough for Walt Disney, one that began an entertainment empire that has brought happiness to millions of people. Walt often said, "We must always remember, it all started with a mouse."

That was how it started, but over the years of Walt's career, other characters were born (or given new life) by the Disney studio, characters that have found their way into the hearts of people around the world: Donald Duck, the Seven Dwarfs, Pluto, Goofy, Bambi, Thumper, Tigger, the Three Little Pigs and so on.

The advent of Disneyland presented Walt with another opportunity to showcase his characters. As everyone knows, people in the costumes of familiar animated friends stroll around the park for guests to meet and greet in person. Children yell and scream and rush up to Mickey, throwing their arms around his spindly legs. He is certainly the most venerated mouse on earth!

A man by the name of Paul Castle played Mickey Mouse at Disneyland for many, many years. He could regale you for hours with stories about his unusual experiences with guests. He once told Mike, "It's hard to be me after I've been Mickey all day!" He loved his job, but he also considered it a real learning opportunity. Mike and Disney executive Bob Mathieson decided that everyone going through the organization's management development program should spend a day in costume portraying one of the characters at Disneyland.

It's an amazing experience to be inside the costume of a Disney character. You're treated differently. Suddenly, people are approachable, because *you* are approachable. The facades and personality screens you typically wear begin to melt away. Unspoken threats and quiet mistrust disappear. No one on either side of the mask is worried anymore.

It's very exciting to follow the Disneyland band down Main Street as a spectator, but to be a *character* prancing along the parade route is a truly mind-boggling event for the initiate. This is a unique opportunity to be something different, to be a fantasy creation. It causes people to break out of the box!

A member of one management development group, a man we'll call Ed, had such a transforming experience while playing one of the Three Little Pigs. Ed was a top young manager at Disneyland. He had superb technical skills, but his people skills were limited. He was the perfect candidate for learning some valuable lessons from the character costume experience.

Ed dressed up in his pig costume and made his way through the park with Mike, who was dressed as Baloo, the bear from *The Jungle Book*. Ed was easily the most "animated" Disney character on Main Street that day. Mike will never forget the experience of watching him.

Ed was simply beside himself. There he was—jumping, turning, twisting and dancing as if he had been magically transformed into his character. This rather conservative, technically-minded manager had simply *flipped out* once he donned his pig costume!

Parading about with the band is very hot work, requiring those in costume to go backstage and remove their masks about every half-hour to cool down. At one point, Mike saw Ed cooling down, with the head of his pig costume off and a towel wrapped around his neck to absorb the sweat streaming down his face. But he was sporting the biggest grin Mike had ever seen, and every now and then he would shout, "I *love* it! I just *love* it!"

Mike went over to him and asked, "What is it you love, Ed?"

"The way I'm feeling right now," he said. "I've never felt this way before. I finally know what it is to have people actually like you, to have little kids walk up to you and smile, just like that, without your having to do anything first. It's a great experience. I'd give anything if I could feel like this all the time."

217

Mike asked, "Could I teach you how to feel like you're feeling now all the time, Ed?" (Mike believes in asking permission before making such suggestions.)

Ed said, "Yes! I want to know."

"The way to keep feeling the way you feel right now," Mike explained, "is to *think* like you're thinking right now. This experience has caused you to think differently now than you usually do."

Ed stared at Mike, thought for a moment, then nodded his head and grinned an even bigger grin than before. He'd gotten it. At that moment, he'd started his own revival. At that moment, he broke out of the box.

From that day on, Ed took courses on leadership, the psychology of personal relationships and just about any other topic he could find to inspire himself and upgrade his social skills. The result: a new man who was a well-rounded, effective executive. As a matter of fact, Ed went on to become one of the top executives in the Disney organization, running a vital company subsidiary. Ed's vicarious breakthrough experience as a Disney character led to a breakthrough *during* and *after* the fact because he *decided* to leave behind his old way of thinking. He *decided* to broaden his skills. He *decided* to transform himself.

Looking at the mountaintop

Some time ago, we visited Disneyland to attend the character parade at the sundown retreat ceremony. We revisited some of Mike's old haunts while he was dean of Disney University. For a brief moment, they could even see the "ghosts of parades past" walking down Main Street toward Sleeping Beauty's Castle—U.S. presidents, Card Walker, Roy Disney, Ed in his Three Little Pigs suit, Jack Nicklaus, Cary Grant...and, of course, Mickey, Donald and their friends, including literally millions of guests. All of these special guests seemed present somehow as we surveyed the park. And one more person worth mentioning seemed to be in attendance, too.

Legend has it that Walt Disney watches the retreat ceremony and flag-lowering every night from the top of the Matterhorn Mountain. There are only a few people who can see him up there, waving to the passersby in the street below. It is our hope that you will see Walt the next time you look at the top of the Matterhorn Mountain—or the top of any mountain you need to scale.

Only a few people let their imaginations soar enough to *break out of the box* and see what remains hidden to others. You can be one of them.

Break out of the box!

INDEX

Think Out of the Box
by **Mike Vance** and **Diane Deacon**

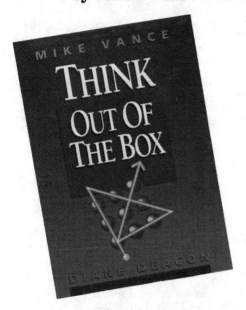

To solve any problem in today's fast-changing global marketplace, companies need people who aren't "boxed in" by traditional modes of thinking, who approach situations with innovative solutions.

Drawing on his own creative expertise as the former dean of Disney University and as in-demand corporate adviser and speaker, Mike Vance uses a nine-dot matrix to plot the nine necessary points of a creative culture. He and coauthor Diane Deacon show you how to connect these components and make them part of *your* company's culture. Together they tell you how to turn your own ways of thinking upside down...so you can turn your organization right side up.

Order your copy of *Think Out of the Box,* today!

Just call toll-free, 1-800-227-3371 (in N.J., 201-848-0310).
You may use MasterCard or Visa. Allow three weeks for delivery.

Or complete and mail the order form below.
Include a check or pay by credit card. Allow four weeks for delivery.

✂ cut here ✂